THE VILLAS OF EDGERTON

HOME TO HUDDERSFIELD'S VICTORIAN ELITE

DAVID GRIFFITHS

original photography by
ANDREW CAVENEY

The Villas of Edgerton: home to Huddersfield's Victorian elite

This edition first published in 2017
by Huddersfield Civic Society
3 Booth Bank, Huddersfield HD7 5XA

British Library Cataloguing-in-Publication

942.813
The villas of Edgerton : home to Huddersfield's Victorian elite /
David Griffiths ; photographed by Andrew Caveney.
—Huddersfield : Huddersfield Civic Society, 2017. —1 volume
: illustrations ; 21 cm
ISBN 9780995632813 (pbk.) : £12.95
BNB Number GBB775240
    Edgerton (Huddersfield, England), History.
    Edgerton (Huddersfield, England), Buildings, structures,
etc.
Prepublication record

ISBN 978-0-9956328-1-3

Printed in England by Riasca, Enterprise Works, Long Lane,
Honley, Holmfirth HD9 6EA

Text, cover design and layout by Paul Buckley of Riasca

Contents

Publisher's Foreword   1

Foreword   3

Preface & Acknowledgements   4

Introduction   7

Edgerton before 1800   11

Georgian Edgerton   17

The Birth of the Victorian Suburb   23
    The release of the land   24
    The development process   31

The Built Character of the Suburb   37
    Architects   42

Edgerton Society   45
    Manufacturers   45
    Merchant princes   48
    Professionals and tradesmen   49
    Public and private life   50

Completing the Suburb   59
    The public domain   59
    Changes in the housing market   62
    Fin-de-siecle opulence   63
    Edgerton in 1911   68

Perambulation	75
Edgerton Grove Road	75
Edgerton Road	78
The Villas of Edgerton (map)	84
Cleveland Road	95
Halifax Road & Hungerford Road	98
Thornhill Road and beyond	109
Edgerton Park & Kaffir Road	114
Bryan Road, Binham Road & Rose Hill	119
Queen's Road & Murray Road	132
Notes	143
Table of Houses	151
Index	157
Picture Credits	164

Publisher's Foreword

2017 IS THE 50th anniversary of the Civic Amenities Act 1967, which introduced the concept and establishment of conservation areas.

Edgerton was designated as a conservation area in 1976, when it was recognised as an "area of special architectural or historic interest, the character and appearance of which it is desirable to preserve and enhance". Edgerton is one of 11 conservation areas in Huddersfield which help preserve and enhance the quality of life in the town. Conservation in Huddersfield has acted as a catalyst for regeneration, helping to diversify the economic base and enhance the character and appearance of the areas, ensuring that the heritage of the town is both a historic and economic asset.

Civic Voice has been encouraging its member civic societies to take part in its 2017 Conservation Conversation. Huddersfield Civic Society is proud to publish this book as our contribution to Civic Day 2017 as we reflect upon the history, review the current position and share our concerns and hopes for the future of our conservation areas.

The book was generously offered to the Society for publication by its author, David Griffiths. We thank him for his years of careful research and writing. To have the professionalism and enthusiasm of local photographer Andrew Caveney of Creative Digital Photography and the graphic skills of Dean Meacham on maps, both illustrating and supporting the text, has been very valuable.

For permission to reproduce other illustrations, we are grateful to the British Newspaper Archive, Alan Brooke, Elaine Ellam, Martin Freeman, Alan Godfrey Maps, Linda Hepworth, Historic England Archive, the Hopkinson, Bunting & Moore families, Sir P H Kaye Bt, Kirklees Council (Libraries and Planning Services), Kirklees Image Archive, the Royal Institute of British Architects, Simon Broadbent, Thornhill Yorkshire Estates, Stan Walker and West Yorkshire Archive Service – Kirklees.

The book has been generously sponsored by Boultons Estate Agency which has allowed us to make the book affordable. The Institute of Historic Building Conservation's Conservation Areas Anniversary Fund gave us a handsome grant to cover the cost of scanning and publication rights of Historic England Archive images. Historic England Archive responded by giving us a discount in recognition of the significance of the Conservation Conversation. I thank them all for their kind support.

Such a work is never complete. The author and publisher would be pleased to receive corrections, supplementary information and images. We can be reached through our website www.huddersfieldcivicsociety.org.uk or by email info@huddersfieldcivicsociety.org.uk

BERNARD AINSWORTH
President, Huddersfield Civic Society

Foreword

EDGERTON WAS A quintessential upper-middle class Victorian suburb. Its villas, built up-wind of Huddersfield town centre in their own grounds – detached or made to appear so – on rising land about a mile or so from the cloth hall were ideally placed to house the town's elite of manufacturers, merchants and professionals. Here they could be private with their families and yet also part of a network of power and influence over those who lived and worked in the meaner streets below. Remarkably much of Edgerton still survives to give meaning to the phrase 'leafy suburb'.

In this book David Griffiths does a double service. First, he provides a history of Edgerton, its rise and its prime, introducing the landlords whose restrictive covenants secured the unique character of the area, the developers, the architects, and above all the families who bought or rented their homes there. Drawing on his previous research into the Huddersfield elite this section enhances our understanding not only of the suburb but of the people and their relationships with one another and with the social, economic and political development of the town.

Secondly, in the latter half of the work we are provided with a guide book to enable us to walk through this patch of living history, this one-time oasis of wealth and power, savouring its still largely tranquil atmosphere and appreciating the physical opulence of a bygone age. This is a book for the serious student of social geography or domestic architecture and at the same time an ideal companion for the Huddersfield resident with an afternoon to spare and a curiosity about the history of the town and how its one-time leaders once lived.

PROFESSOR EDWARD ROYLE
Emeritus Professor of History
University of York

Preface & Acknowledgements

LIVING IN EDGERTON since 1989, I have been gathering information about the district's history for many years. It has been a long-standing ambition to shape this material into a publication. For their help in achieving this, three people deserve special thanks.

The late John Brook's 1979 typescript, 'The development of the Edgerton district of Huddersfield during the 19th century – with particular reference to the people who lived there' (housed in Huddersfield Local Studies Library) was an indispensable starting point – indeed without his groundwork, the task might have proved too daunting, and one motivation has been to bring his research to a wider audience. Huddersfield Civic Society chair Christopher Marsden has given tireless and enthusiastic support to the project, going far beyond his duties as publisher to supplement (and sometimes correct) my knowledge of Edgerton's residents and to track down historical illustrations from around the globe. And Andrew Caveney's fine contemporary photographs complement and enrich the text at every turn.

I have consulted a wide range of printed and archival material. Standard sources to describe family history, notably the Census and local newspapers, have not been separately referenced, but specific quotations and archival sources are referenced in the endnotes. The services and staff of Huddersfield Local Studies Library and West Yorkshire Archive Service have been indispensable in navigating the sources.

For more specific help of many kinds, including permission for photography, I am also grateful to Jonathan Adamson, Kamran Ali, Rosamond Allwood, Alwoodleigh Residential Home, Ishrat Amini, Robert Barrett, Christine Beacham, Clyde Binfield, Peter Bissell, David Blakeborough, David Bowen, Alan Brooke, Robert Broughan, William Crowther, Anthony Dann, Pradeep Das, Stan Driver, Brian du Feu, David & Janet Ellis, Alyson Etherington, David Faulder, Fibre Architects, Veronica Foster-McBride, Simon Goodyear, Charlotte Grayson, Haliza Haniff, Norma Hardy, David Harpin, Linda Hepworth, David Hollingworth, Tosca Howe, Huddersfield Ukrainian Club, John Kybaluk, Jeff Lloyd, Roger Lynch, Shona Malcolm, Richard Marczewski, Dean Meacham, Penny Miller, Nivin & Ray Milne, Chris Moore, Denis Murphy, Angi Naylor, Jake Norris, Deborah Orlopp, Jennifer Preston, Raymond Prior, George Redmonds, Grant & Shirley Roberts, Sadeh Lok Housing Group, Joseph Sharples, Mike & Marina Shaw, Socrates Psychological Services, Kerry Simpson, Robert Sutcliffe, Angela Sykes, Edmund Thornhill, Alan Tinsdeall, Sarah Towers, Christine Verguson, David Verguson, John Ward, Chris Woods, Nicholas & Marie-Christine Wright, David Wyles, Andy & Sandy Young and, with apologies, to anyone I have overlooked.

John Brook, John Eastwood, Brian Haigh, Martin Kilburn, Edward Royle, Jane Griffiths, Christopher Marsden and William Murgatroyd have read and commented on drafts of the text, with Martin Kilburn doing particular service by 'road-testing' the walking tour in the second half of the book. Any errors which remain are of course my own responsibility.

The project has regularly threatened to get out of hand. To keep it to manageable proportions, I have limited the focus to what I see as the 'classic' Edgerton of substantial Victorian houses in spacious garden settings – a good deal less than the whole of the Edgerton Conservation Area. With few exceptions, too, the story ends with the First World War; one day somebody may want to write a 20th century sequel.

The structure of the book is simple: a general narrative is followed by a house-by-house 'perambulation' (to use architectural historian Sir Nikolaus Pevsner's splendid term). I hope the price paid in occasional duplication of material does not prove too high: the challenge as ever is to organise the facts into a good story.

I dedicate the book to Jacob, Effie and Max, whose stories have just begun.

DAVID GRIFFITHS
April 2017

Edgerton Conservation Area

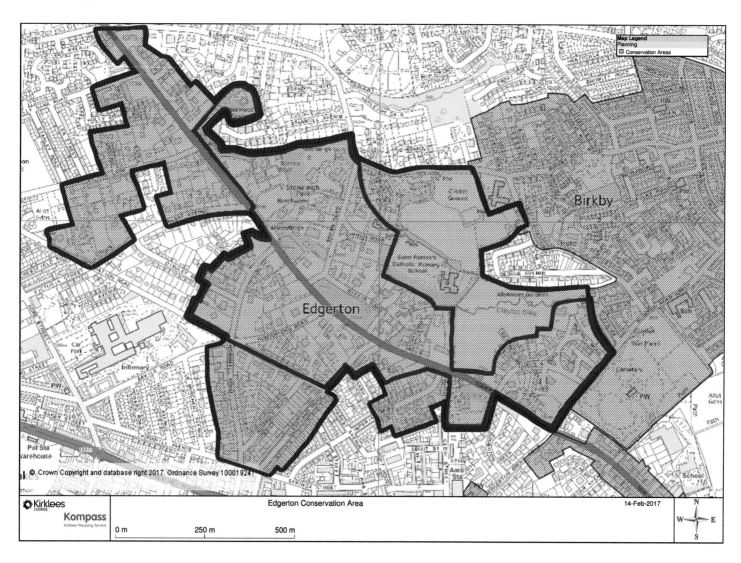

Introduction

A MILE OR so north-west of Huddersfield town centre, amongst dense tree cover along the main road to Halifax, lies the district of Edgerton. It is a remarkably well-preserved example of the Victorian villa suburb. Indeed the architectural historian of West Yorkshire, Derek Linstrum, suggests that Edgerton "can be recognised as the essence of the middle-class suburban ideal, in which buildings and settings merge into a picturesque whole which nevertheless respects each man's individuality and privacy."[1] There has been infill development throughout the 20th century, and of course much change of use, from large single-family homes to a more varied mix today, including apartment living, multi-occupation, business and institutional use. But there have been only a handful of demolitions – unlike much-celebrated Victoria Park in Manchester, or Adel in Leeds, Edgerton is very largely intact. Moreover recent years have seen a trend to return its houses from nursing homes and other institutions to private residential use.

Edgerton's special character was recognised by Kirklees Council in 1976 when it declared the Edgerton Conservation Area (ECA). This covered 81 hectares and, as the designation report acknowledged, extends well beyond what any resident would regard as 'Edgerton', taking in substantial parts of Marsh, Lindley and Birkby. It was reviewed in 2007 and the boundaries (blue on fig.1) somewhat tightened, with six distinct 'character areas' identified. Just one of these, Character Area 1 (red on the map), is the Edgerton heartland and the focus of this book. Around half of the total area, this includes 85 of the ECA's 98 listed building entries (set out in the Table, pp.151–6) – a remarkable total, though admittedly almost half are modest structures such as gate piers and walls. Except for Edgar Wood's (Edwardian) Banney Royd, listed at grade I, the listings are all at grade II.

Fig.1
Edgerton Conservation Area (blue boundary) and, within it, Character Area 1 (red boundary). To the east are the Birkby and (bottom right) Greenhead Park conservation areas.

Despite later additions and a tiny Georgian residue, Edgerton is very largely a creation of the third quarter of the 19th century. The years around 1850 have long been recognised as a turning point in British history, when the intense economic, social and political growing pains of the 'Industrial Revolution' gave way to a period of mid-Victorian prosperity, political stability and social complacency. The 1851 Great Exhibition, showcasing the country's unchallenged if short-lived status as 'workshop of the world', epitomises the moment.

Local history neatly fits this template, and provides the background to Edgerton's development. The first half of the 19th century had seen

Huddersfield's transition from market village to industrial town, with fourfold population growth, a crisis of insanitary working-class housing and intense political conflicts, from the Luddite uprising of 1812 through Richard Oastler's campaigns for the Factory Acts and against the New Poor Law to the Chartist agitation of the 1840s.

In contrast to all of this was the rapid emergence of a new civic culture from the late 1840s. Work on the railway station began in 1846, offering services to Leeds, Manchester and Sheffield by 1850. This enabled the rapid development of the 'new town', centred on St George's Square and largely comprising commercial offices and warehouses, through the 1850s. At the same time the 1848 Huddersfield Improvement Act swept away the struggling local government agencies of the previous 30 years, replacing them with a new body, the Huddersfield Improvement Commissioners, armed with much more extensive powers (though fully modern local government would wait until 1868). The town's two newspapers, the Tory *Chronicle* and Liberal *Examiner*, were founded in 1850 and 1851; the Chamber of Commerce in 1852. The 1850s also saw several major mill developments as the transition from the domestic to the factory system proceeded apace. As Jane Springett explains, with the advent of the railway:

> Merchants and manufacturers found that they no longer needed to invest in large stocks and the more prominent members of the community sought to capitalize on the fruits of the early century and turned their minds to personal conspicuous consumption in the form of increasing living space.[2]

For these businessmen, and the professionals on whom they depended, many of them also the leading figures in new public institutions, Edgerton was the natural place to make a new home – close to the town but upwind from its smoke on the westerly slopes, largely undeveloped and, as we shall see, with extensive land coming onto the market to meet the demand. But Edgerton did not spring from nothing in the 1850s: it had a prior history which we should briefly relate.

Fig.2
View of Huddersfield by William Cowen, painted in 1849 as Edgerton's development took off. On the left horizon are the wooded slopes which would soon become the Victorian suburb.

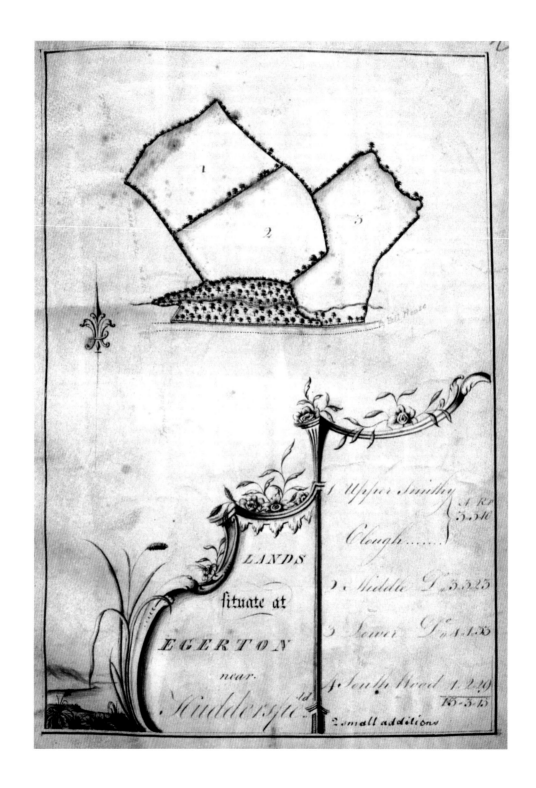

LANDS

situate at

EGERTON

near.

Huddersfield

1 Upper Smithy &

Clough........

2 Middle D.º 3.3.23

3 Lower D.º 1.1.35

4 South Wood 1.2.20

15.3.15

2 small additions

Edgerton before 1800

WHAT WE NOW know as Edgerton straddles the old townships of Huddersfield and Lindley, but before the mid-19th century it was strictly a Huddersfield place name. Its first recorded appearance is in 1311, when it is said to mean the farmstead of 'Ecgheard'.[3] Noting that this is a Germanic name, however, Dr George Redmonds has suggested a much earlier origin, as a stopping point on the line of advance of Anglian settlers into the district in the 7th century, crossing the Calder at Cooper Bridge and continuing via Deighton, Edgerton and Gledholt rather than following the marshy Colne Valley.[4]

In any event, the documentary record establishes continuous settlement from the 14th century onwards. This seems to have comprised essentially a single farmstead close to the later Edgerton Hill (today's Ukrainian Club on Edgerton Rd). The associated land, growing to perhaps 75 acres by the 16th century, was divided between the manors of Almondbury and Huddersfield. Both of these famously came into the hands of the Ramsden family, in 1599 and 1631 respectively, with momentous consequences for Huddersfield history, but Edgerton survived as a separate if short-lived manor, before being divided into several small freehold estates in the late C18 (see p.17). The Ramsdens therefore played no direct role in Edgerton's development, and of much greater significance for the future, as we shall see, was the purchase of the manor of Lindley and Quarmby by Thomas Thornhill in 1634.[5]

The first large scale map to depict the area was drawn up with reference to a Ramsden estate survey in 1780 (though the map itself, fig.3 must date from the 1790s, as it includes some later changes of ownership).[6] This shows the farmstead of Edgerton comprising three buildings, accessed by a side turning from what is now Edgerton Grove Rd (previously Blacker Lane).

Fig.3
Fenton estate map of 1780 – the fields now occupied by Queen's Rd and Murray Rd and Blacker Lane Wood.

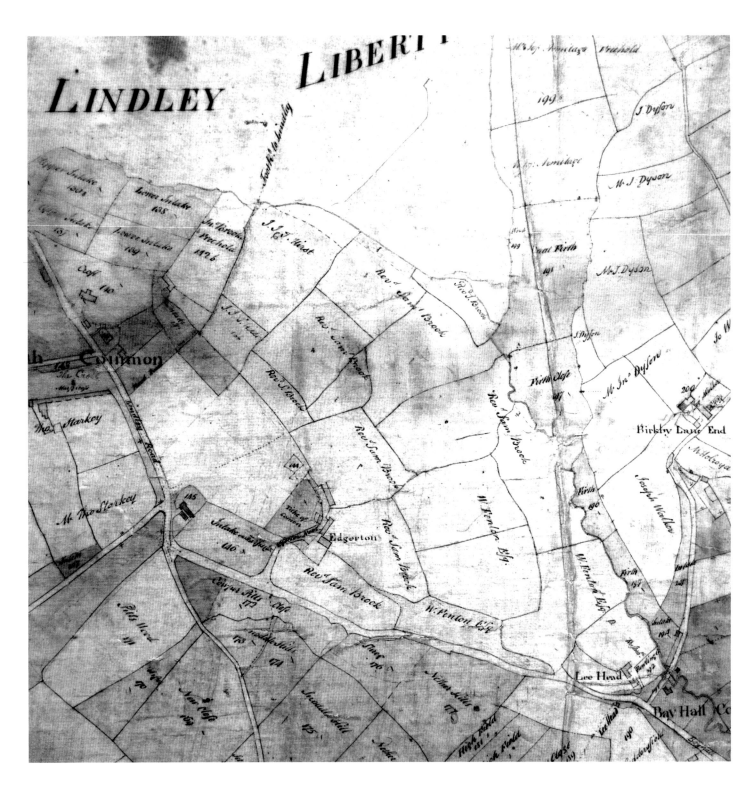

Fig.4
Ramsden estate map of the 1790s, original and redrawn. Above 'Gledholt' is today's junction of Westbourne Rd and Blacker Rd at the Gledholt roundabout. On the right, the 'dog leg' line of today's Birkby Lodge Rd can be seen. Between these landmarks, the absence of today's Halifax road is evident.

It lies at the southern end of a substantial land-holding by Revd Sam Brook, running north to the Clayton Dike. To the west are plots owned by brothers John, Joseph & Thomas Hirst, and to the east by W Fenton esquire.

At the time Samuel Brook was rector of Friern Barnet, Middlesex and lived in Surrey. Despite his distant location, he had strong connections with

Huddersfield. His father, almost certainly, was also Revd Samuel Brook, curate of Flockton and master of King James's Grammar School at Almondbury, while his brother Edward, an apothecary, had married Elizabeth Firth of Clough House, Birkby. Her father Abraham was connected with Edgerton earlier in the C18 and it may be that the Brook land holdings there derived from the Clough House estate.[7]

Having moved south, however, Revd Brook was evidently disposing of his Huddersfield land by the late C18. By the time of the map, the Fentons and the Hirsts had already purchased their holdings from him, in 1778 and 1784 respectively.[8] Further attempted sales on Brook's death in 1794 and 1801 (fig.5) brought to market the Edgerton farmstead itself and the land around it.[9] Promoted to a 'mansion house' in these sale adverts, it may have been known as Armytage or Armitage House – the occupier in 1794 was one William Armytage, a cloth dresser – and there is a later reference to Armitage Wood, in a press report of an 1837 murder.[10]

Off the map to the north west, beyond the Sunny Bank Beck, which follows today's Cleveland Rd, lay Lindley, where the Thornhill estate was the principal landowner (see p.26). On their land too was a substantial Georgian house, Sunny Bank, still partly standing today, at the corner of Sunnybank Rd and Cleveland Rd. This came to Thomas Hirst in the 1798 Lindley enclosure award.

With these two exceptions, however, at the turn of the C18 today's Edgerton was a typical South Pennine landscape of small fields and woodlands, incised by the deep ravines of the Clayton Dike, Sunny Bank Beck and several smaller streams. In this respect little had changed since 1584, when the Almondbury Manor Inquisition described the settlement thus:

> Edward Cowper holdeth one messuage called Edgerton, lying within the township of Huddersfield, one garden, one orchard, two little meadows called the Crofts, with a little spring of wood at the end thereof, one close called the Nethermost field, one close called the 'Smithy Clough', one meadow called Bonging now divided in two, one close called 'Wheatfield', one close called the nether middle field, one close called the overmiddlefield, one little meadow called the Hoyleing,

one little meadow called herdplatt, one close called Longlands now divided into two, one close called the overmost field and two little closes called Smithie closes with a little cottage thereupon builded and one parcel of ground called Smithie Hoyle freely by socage and rent by year vi'd [6 pence].[11]

Egerton, near Huddersfield,

To be SOLD by AUCTION,

On Thursday the Twenty-second Day of October last, betwixt the Hours of Four and Seven o'Clock in the Afternoon of the same Day, if not sold in the mean While by private Contract, of which Notice will be given, at Mr. John Booth's, the Rose and Crown Inn, Huddersfield,

(In the following, or divided into such Lots as will be most agreeable to the Purchasers,)

Lot I. ALL that FREEHOLD MANSION or DWELLING-HOUSE, with the Barn, Stables, Cowhouse, and other Outbuildings, Garden, Foldstead, &c. together with the Tenement and Outbuildings occupied by Thomas Beaumont, Pres-shop adjoining thereto, with a Cottage and Garden, in the Occupation of John Todd, together with Two Closes of Land adjoining the said Mansion-House, called the Grannam Croft and House Ing, with the New Inclosure Piece, containing together Six Acres, One Rood, and Fifteen Perches, be the same more or less; also One Pew in the Parish Church of Huddersfield.

Lot II. TWO CLOSES of Rich and very Valuable LAND, commonly called the Lower Long Close and the Thornton Ing, with the Shrogg adjoining thereto, containing together Eight Acres, Three Roods and Fourteen Perches, be the same more or less, with a Road through Clover Close reserved to the same.

Lot III. A DWELLING-HOUSE, in the Occupation of John Marshall, Sen. and John Marshall, Jun. a Cottage in James Giles's Occupation, an Old Barn and Butcher's Shop, Two Gardens, with a Close of Land adjoining, called the Clover Close, containing Three Acres, Two Roods and Twenty-five Perches, be the same more or less, reserving a Road through the said Close to other Premises adjoining thereto; also One Pew in Huddersfield Church, in the Occupation of the Rev. Mr. Withnell.

Lot IV. THREE CLOSES of LAND, in the Occupation of Mr. John Booth, and Thomas Beaumont, called or known by the several Names of the Burnt Close, Long Close, and the Hoyle Ing, containing Seven Acres Two Roods and Twenty-six Perches, be the same more or less, with a Road reserved through the Bottom of the Bean Close to the same.

Lot V. THREE CLOSES of LAND, in the Occupation of Mr. John Booth, and Thomas Beaumont, with the Wood adjoining, called the Bean Close, Round Field, and Further Four Days Work, containing Seven Acres Three Roods and Thirty-four Perches, be the same more or less, reserving a Road over the Bottom of Bean Close to Lot Fourth into Burnt Close.

Lot VI. A COTTAGE, in the Occupation of James Dyson.

☞ The above Estate is Tythe Free, known to contain both Stone and Coal, most delightfully situated within One Mile of the Town of Huddersfield, and in the Centre of a Manufacturing Country.

John Marshall, Jun. will shew the Premises; and for further Particulars apply to Mr. Samuel Brook, of Mirfield; Mr. Richard Brook, of Leeds; Mr. Edward Brook, Attorney at Law, in Wakefield; or of Mr. Sykes, Attorney at Law, in Dewsbury.

Fig.5
Sale particulars for the Edgerton farmstead in 1801.

EDGERTON GROVE HUDDERSFIEL

Georgian Edgerton

THE DISPOSAL OF the Brook lands brought new freeholders to historic Edgerton. The Fentons eventually developed their land as today's Queen's and Murray Roads – but not until the 1860s. The initial purchase by the Hirst brothers would become the Croft House estate at neighbouring Marsh, not developed until the late C19. But the Hirsts went on to buy more of the Brook land, closer to the Edgerton settlement, as did the Robinsons of Birkby Grange (who acquired Clayton Fields) and, of most immediate significance, John Battye and his brother-in-law Frederick Hudson. (See p.25 for a map of the various land ownerships by the mid-C19.)

Fig.6
The drive of Edgerton Grove, off Blacker Lane (now Edgerton Grove Rd) around 1900.

Fig.7
The historic Edgerton Lane, surviving today off Glebe St (and located in fig.8 overleaf).

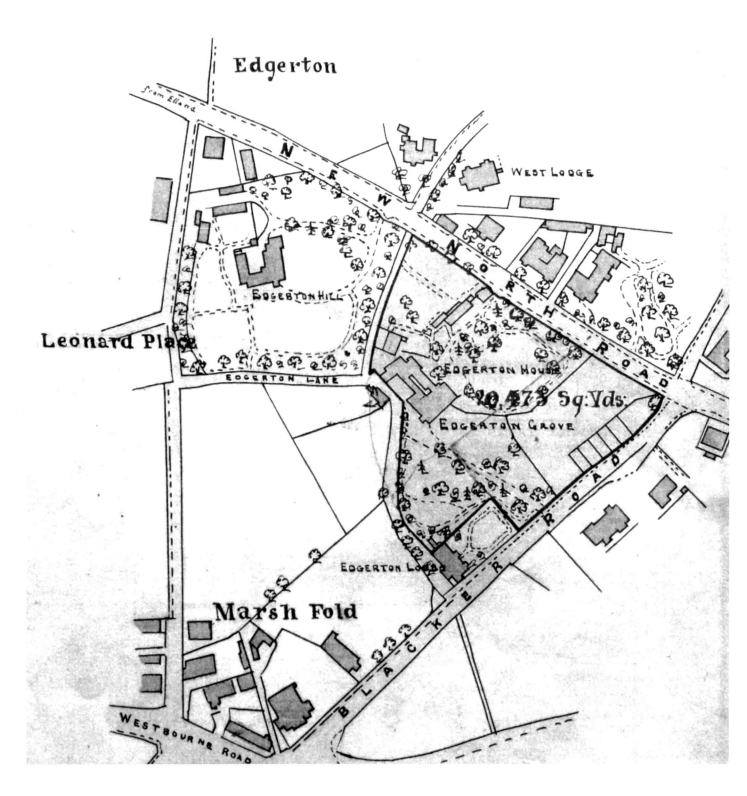

John Battye was a solicitor in Huddersfield – indeed, a member of the great clan of inter-related Battyes, Croslands and Fentons who dominated the town's legal affairs in the 18th and early 19th centuries. He had married Elizabeth Hudson, whose brother Frederick was a linen draper. Both men were members of an increasingly prosperous class of retailers and professionals in the growing town, and together bought the land around the historic Edgerton settlement in 1813.[12] By about 1820 the earlier farmstead was replaced by a small Georgian suburb, comprising four substantial dwellings.[13] The plan opposite (fig.8) depicts it in 1897.

Edgerton Hill, today's Ukrainian Club, first occupied by Hudson himself, is discussed below in the 'perambulation' (p.82). The other houses were demolished in the 1960s to make way for today's Edgerton Green housing estate. Near to Edgerton Hill was Edgerton House, soon – if not always – divided, with the smaller part named Edgerton Grove, while alongside Blacker Lane (now Edgerton Grove Rd) was Edgerton Lodge. We can assume that all three properties were in the plain Georgian style still evident, at Edgerton Hill.[14]

Edgerton Lodge was built by a plumber and glazier, Richard Newhouse, who was soon bankrupt. From 1821–25 it was rented by Revd Henry John Maddock, the first incumbent at nearby Holy Trinity Church and after him by other clergymen. One of these, Revd John Gilderdale, a curate at the parish church, ran a school there for boys aged 9 to 15, and fifteen pupils were in residence on Census night in 1841; the school attracted national press coverage six months earlier when two boys died from bonfire night fireworks injuries. In the early 1840s the house was taken by George Henry Brook, who moved to Edgerton Cottage in 1852 (see p.86), and then by James Liebreich (see p.80). The freehold came to auction in 1868 and until 1915 it was home to Colonel Frederick Greenwood, long-standing doctor at the Infirmary.

After John Battye's death in 1837, **Edgerton House & Grove** was bought in 1839 by Thomas Varley, a corn merchant and flour miller at Shore Foot, who served on many of the town's public bodies over a long career. His land extended to the other side of the main road, where its release later aided

Fig.8
Sale plan for the Edgerton Grove estate in 1897. Today's Edgerton Rd appears as 'New North Road' and Bremen House as 'West Lodge'. The ancient lane running south to meet Edgerton Lane, between Edgerton Hill and Edgerton House (now demolished) is walled up and overgrown but still visible.

Fig.9
Revd Henry Maddock, early occupier of Edgerton Lodge.

the growth of the Victorian suburb (see p.28). At the time of purchase, the Grove was occupied by wool merchant and manufacturer Sidney Norris, who moved on to Fixby Hall, and the House by Battye's widow, but the latter soon became Varley's own home. After his death in 1875 and Mrs Varley's in 1880, it was occupied by the long-serving Ramsden estate official Isaac Hordern, whose 63 years in their employ ended in 1909; he died, aged 82, in 1912. Occupiers of Edgerton Grove after Norris included wool merchant Jacob Susmann, who died in 1852; the solicitor Thomas Clough, first clerk to the Improvement Commissioners; and Robert Holliday, son of chemical pioneer Read Holliday (see p.47).

These four polite Georgian homes represented the final incarnation of Edgerton as a small settlement just off the historic axis of Blacker Lane. No sooner were they built, however, than their situation would be changed for ever. The turnpike road between Huddersfield and Halifax had been established in the 1770s along what is now Halifax Old Rd, on the north side of the Grimescar valley. But in 1823 a new route was surveyed on the south side, taking a direct line from Temple St (at the top of Westgate) to Ainley Top – today's New North Rd, Edgerton Rd and Halifax Rd – and the necessary Act of Parliament was passed in 1825.[15] This had profound implications for future development by opening up the land further out to ready access from town.

Still owned by Varley's trustees after his death and let out, at auction in 1897 Edgerton House & Grove were valued mainly for the site – the House was "very old and straggling, very damp", while the Grove was "now unoccupied and altogether out of repair".[16] At that point, however, they were bought by Horace Broadbent of Thomas Broadbent Ltd, the pioneering electrical engineers, who lived at the Grove until his death in 1942. Later still, part of the Lodge was briefly occupied by James Hanson (the future Lord Hanson of Edgerton) after his marriage in 1959 and consequent move from the family home further out at Norwood Grange (see p.66) – though as his card also advertised addresses in Mayfair, Manhattan and Ontario, and he was soon gone, it may be doubted how much time he spent there.[17] Edgerton Hill, in owner-occupation from the start, fared better; by 1839 it

Fig.10
Horace Broadbent of Edgerton Grove.

Fig.11
Edgerton Hill, Edgerton Rd, now
Huddersfield Ukrainian Club.

was the Edgerton 'seat' of the Armitage family, described by John Brook as "the senior family in the district" for most of the C19 (see p.46), and it stands today.

The Birth of the Victorian Suburb

THE NEW TURNPIKE made little impact until the late 1840s, when the growing demand for middle-class housing, discussed above, met a supply of newly-available land. As a former pupil at Huddersfield College recalled, contrasting the scene 40 years on with that in 1838:

> The road to Edgerton and beyond is now flanked by modern villas, the glorious horse-chestnut trees, with their scented blossoms, are things of the past – the streamlet in the valley below, once so pellucid and attractive, is a filthy watercourse...[18]

The 1854 6-inch Ordnance Survey map (fig.12) based on an 1848–50 survey, shows 'Georgian Edgerton' in place but just two new houses further out on the main road – Edgerton Cottage and Edgerton Villa.[19] Beyond that the only marked features are Woodfield Cottage below Sunny Bank; tenter fields between Sunny Bank and the main road; and the Hope beerhouse at 'Daisy Lea Lane Bottom', more Lindley than Edgerton.

A rising middle-class was not of course an overnight creation in 1850. In the years around 1800 merchants had built some substantial houses in the town centre, as the New St/Buxton Rd axis developed. Then a small middle-class enclave grew up in the Highfields area from the 1820s, after the release of Thomas Bradley's estate at Newhouse.[20] This came to comprise Newhouse itself, Bath Buildings (today's Bath St), Brunswick Place and Belgrave Terrace, a handsome curving late-Georgian row of town houses still facing New North Rd just below Huddersfield College – itself built in 1838, and now part of Kirklees College.[21] (On the doorstep of the town centre, in a way which the great cutting of the ring road now makes hard

Fig.12
The 1854 six-inch Ordnance Survey map (surveyed 1848-50), showing early Edgerton (bottom right) in its rural setting. (Reproduced here at approx. 1:10,800.)

to imagine, Highfields is well worth a visit to absorb the atmosphere of what remains.)

Like Edgerton, however, New North Rd remained undeveloped, from the old Infirmary of 1831 – more recently the main Huddersfield site of Kirklees College – to the toll bar at Blacker Lane, until the 1850s. Then it was built up quickly and profusely, as is critically recalled in a contemporary comment:

> …had a little more taste, forethought and judgment been brought to bear, Huddersfield could have been the finest town in England. I say nothing of the Halifax-road, because that is too bewildering an affair to cope with. No one can, however, complain of want of variety in the style of the houses; for there you have Grecian Temples, Swiss Cottages, Gothic Castles, and Italian Villas – all jumbled so closely together as scarcely to allow elbow-room.[22]

New North Rd and Highfields merit their own celebration; but it is precisely this close-packed urban character which sharply distinguishes them from Edgerton beyond the brow of the hill, where the Victorian 'battle of the styles' was set to continue.

The release of the land

IN 1850 THE lands beyond Blacker Lane, aside from the Georgian enclave already described, were in the hands of seven landowners, five of whom would soon release their land for development. Straddling the turnpike lay the estates of Thomas Varley of Edgerton House (see p.19) and, beyond Edgerton Hill, George Lockwood's estate. North of the main road lay first the Fenton land and then that of Thomas Robinson (today's Clayton Fields). Dwarfing all of these, beyond the steep ravine of the Sunny Bank Beck, lay the extensive Edgerton portion of the Thornhill estate, and to its north land owned by Joshua Tolson of Birkby. Only Clayton Fields would remain unavailable for housing by 1864 – and indeed, with the exception of two 1930s semis, for 150 years after that.

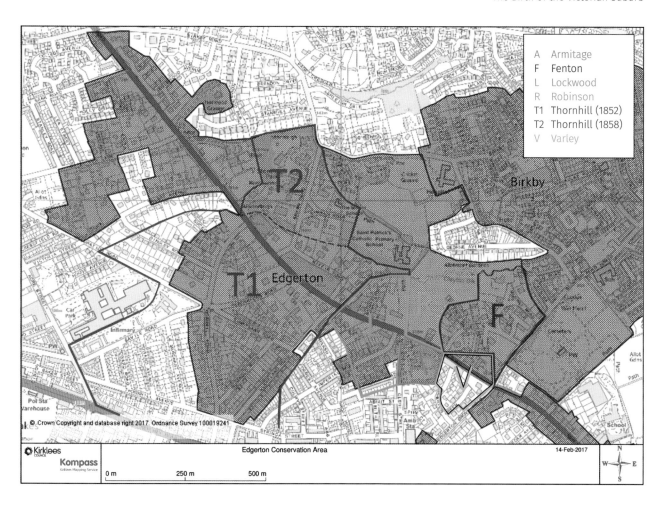

A   Armitage
F   Fenton
L   Lockwood
R   Robinson
T1 Thornhill (1852)
T2 Thornhill (1858)
V   Varley

Fig.13
The relevant land ownership
boundaries of mid-19th
century Edgerton.

First to make a move was **George Lockwood** (L on fig.13). He had married a grand-daughter of John Hirst, one of the three brothers whom we noted earlier buying Revd Brook's land. This branch of the Hirsts lived at Dyke End, an 18th century farmhouse on present-day Portland St, and through his marriage Lockwood evidently inherited a portion of the Hirst estate.[23] Ten substantial houses were soon developed on this land, on both sides of the main road, as well as terraced housing to the south.

The building leases were for 999 years and the first was almost certainly for today's Edgerton Cottage, from 30 January 1847, while those for The Mount and Glenside – the only one to be demolished – ran from 1850.[24] By the time of the 1851 Census, residents were recorded at three of the houses, while the enumerator recorded "six houses building" – a hive of housebuilding activity.

According to his obituary, George Lockwood was "a gentleman of retiring habits, and though often urged declined to take part in public business preferred [sic] a private life. In his younger days however he was fond of shooting."[25] He was however a trustee of the Halifax & Huddersfield turnpike which traversed his property. His land ended at the Sunny Bank Beck, beyond which was the Thornhill estate.

The **Thornhills** were the next to begin to release land (T1 on fig.13) – and on a grand scale. They were a great landed family, linked by marriage to the still grander Saviles, with over 2600 acres in the West Riding by 1873,[26] and they left a profound imprint on the development of Edgerton (and indeed Lindley and Hillhouse too). Their local landholdings went back to a 14th century marriage between Richard de Thornhill and Margaret de Totehill [Toothill, Rastrick], but were much augmented in upper Edgerton by the Lindley Enclosure Award of 1798.[27] The family's seat at Fixby Hall (leased to Huddersfield Golf Club until 2065) probably dates from the same period, and its rebuild in a polite Georgian style around 1780, perhaps with John Carr's involvement, provided the model for several of the 'villa mansions' built in subsequent years for less grand 'nouveau riche' families.[28] From 1800 the family head was another Thomas Thornhill, the fourth of that name, who soon moved away from Fixby to another seat in Norfolk, leaving the Hall and estate in the hands of his steward, Robert Oastler; the latter's son, the 'Tory Radical' Richard, inherited the post in 1820 and famously made it the local base for his campaigning activities.

After Thornhill's death in 1844 his third wife, Honoria, married Henry Hungerford, of Dingley, Northants and decided that neither she nor her two daughters and step-daughter had any further personal use for Fixby or its Lindley estates. (The daughters' names, Clara, Honoria and Eleanor were later adopted for three streets on Thornhill land off Bradford Rd, where a recent development has also been named Three Sisters Square.) Instead it made more sense to release capital from the estate for the benefit of the daughters, all aged under ten when the case began but no doubt requiring handsome marriage settlements in due course.

A major obstacle here was the prohibition in Thomas Thornhill III's will of the alienation of land through building leases – a typical example of the 'strict settlement' by which landed families prevented the break-up of their assets. The years 1844 to 1851 saw a complex case go forward in the Court of Chancery – memorably satirised by Dickens in *Bleak House* – in order to overcome this obstacle.[29] Eventually the court authorised Mrs Hungerford to promote the legislation necessary to 'disentail' the estate. The result was the Thornhill Estate Acts of 1852–5, of which the first was the most important. Its short title was:

> To enable the INFANT TENANTS IN TAIL ... to grant BUILDING and other LEASES, and to Sell or Exchange the same.

Its preamble is evocative of the perceived potential of Huddersfield at this moment of mid-century optimism:

> And whereas as to a considerable portion of the Estates of which the said Clara Thornhill is the tenant in tail general in possession ... the same is situate within 3 miles, or thereabouts, of the town of Huddersfield, in the West Riding of the county of Yorkshire, in which town and in the neighbourhood thereof a large increase of dwellings and of mills and other buildings for manufacturing purposes has taken place within these few years, and there is still a great and increasing demand in the said town and neighbourhood for building sites for the erection as well of mills, manufactories, and other buildings suitable for manufacturing purposes, as also for villas and dwelling houses, and numerous application have been made to the said John Hodgson Ramsbotham [of Fixby Hall], the Receiver in the said cause, for the grant of sites to build upon for the purposes aforesaid ....

... three trustees would be empowered, on behalf of the daughters, to grant 999-year leases on terms set out therein (and which will be reviewed below). The Act gained Royal Assent on 17 July.

A few weeks earlier, on 10 May, there had been an auction of "very important estates at Bay Hall and Birkby".[30] Owned by **Joshua Tolson**, these included the land between today's Kaffir Rd and Birkby Rd (then Long Lane) – regarded then as 'Birkby' but soon to be rebranded 'Upper Edgerton' and developed as Bryan and Binham Roads (T2 on fig.13).[31] Where the Thornhill Estate Act just quoted stressed the economic prosperity of the town, the Tolson particulars of sale emphasised the specific attractions of the site:

> The lots at Birkby are within a few minutes' drive of the important town of Huddersfield, and present 22 Villa sites, which for picturesque beauty cannot be excelled in the surrounding neighbourhood, the same being well wooded, and a considerable stream of Water runs through the Estate which may be diverted for both useful and ornamental purposes.

As this implied, Tolson's agents had prepared a detailed plan for villas, arranged around a cruciform road plan. Despite its charms, the site was not sold on that occasion, but came to market again in 1856, and was added to the Thornhill estate in 1858. (It was actually bought at auction by the local Ramsden agent Thomas Brook, but his action was disavowed by the estate; the chief agent George Loch had earlier taken the view that land in Edgerton "can never be as eligible as New North Road".)[32]

The same year saw **Thomas Varley** release his land nearer to town (V on fig.13) – a triangular plot tapering from Blacker Lane to an apex where Queen's Rd now meets the main road (Edgerton Rd at this point), severed from the grounds of Edgerton House by the turnpike. This was first marketed as 13 lots – 10 along the road, three larger ones behind – and with elevations already prepared by noted architects James Pritchett & Sons (see p.42). Ten houses along the turnpike, whether terraced or closely-packed semis, would have extended the urban pattern of New North Rd into Edgerton. However the auction was immediately postponed and within three weeks a new division into only four plots came to market.[33] It was on these that the substantial villas of Bankfield, Clyde House, Mayfield and Grannum Lodge would soon be built.

Last to join the development boom, but not far behind Lockwood and Thornhill, was the **Fenton estate** (F on fig.13). Once again the Fentons were major local landowners, with over 1300 acres in the 1873 survey. A branch of the Fenton family had moved from Penistone to Huddersfield in the 1730s, renting Greenhead Hall until William Fenton built his own home at Spring Grove in 1791 (demolished in 1879 to make way for Spring Grove School). Their interest in Edgerton derived, as we have seen, from the purchase of the future Queen's Rd/Murray Rd area from Revd. Brook in 1778, which they had surveyed and attractively mapped in 1780 (fig.3, p.10). William Fenton died in 1822 and his Huddersfield estates, also including land at Birkby and Longroyd Bridge, passed to his son Lewis. Elected as Huddersfield's first MP in 1832, the latter met an untimely end falling from a window of Spring Grove in the following year; this ended the male line and the estate passed into the hands of trustees, who had financial commitments to various female members of the family.

In just the same way as the Thornhills, the Fenton trustees turned their minds to enhancing their income through urban development, and faced the same need to 'disentail' the estate. In 1860 their agent, George Crowther, recommended an approach to Chancery to release the Edgerton and Spring Grove estates. A dispute with one of the trust's beneficiaries – a Mrs Eliza Murray, perhaps a grand-daughter of William Fenton – delayed matters for nearly three years, with the trustees at one point recording their "extreme indignation at the vexatious and unnecessary delay" and determination not to be "saddled with the many unnecessary expenses that have been incurred".[34] By this time, however, the demand from landowners for release from inherited legal obligations had become so common that the Settled Estates Act 1856 had been passed to facilitate it. Accordingly, once Chancery had delivered a judgement under this statute, on 16 August 1864, the trustees were free to proceed without the need, like the Thornhills, to promote private legislation.[35]

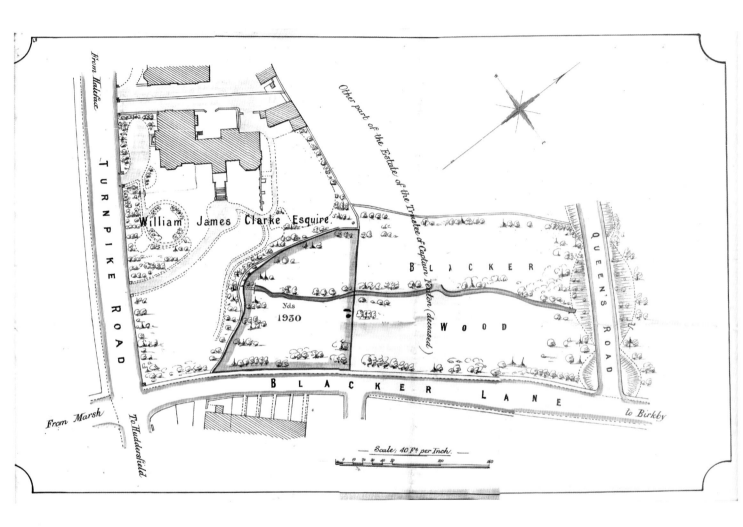

Fig.14
The plan shows Mayfield & Grannum Lodge, Edgerton Rd in 1869. William Clarke had bought his plot from Thomas Varley and was now to lease the extra plot marked in pink, on which a small lodge would be built, from the Fenton estate. The adjoining Fenton land had not yet been developed: Blacker Wood, shown with its stream (now lost), would later become the sunken garden of Ellerslie.

Between 1847 and 1864, therefore, all the land of Edgerton – except for Thomas Robinson's Clayton Fields and the Armitages' Edgerton Hill (R & A on fig.13) – had become available for development. But in the main the landowners retained a firm grip on the nature of that development, which shaped the character of the suburb we know today.

The development process

NONE OF THESE landlords intended to build the houses themselves – all wished to lease the land and leave the building to others. To attract the clients they wanted, therefore, they had to ensure that the terms of lease were set appropriately – the first of these being the length of lease they offered.

This was particularly important because other land on the town's western slopes, owned by the Ramsden estate and still closer to town, was potentially available for development. From the 1840s the Ramsdens, who had long owned most of the town centre – and whose estates dwarfed those even of Thornhill and Fenton – embarked on a land-buying spree, fuelled by the proceeds from the sale of the Ramsden Canal to the new railway company. Purchases of the Bay Hall estate in 1844, Greenhead & Gledholt in 1848 and Springwood in 1861, together with existing land in the New North Rd area, gave the Ramsdens control of an arc of land apparently with huge potential for villa development. By the end of 1847, even before its purchase was completed, Ramsden agent Alexander Hathorn had plans for the street lay-out of Greenhead.[36] In 1850 he commissioned a plan for all the land between the Greenhead and Bay Hall boundaries, and in 1862/3 a further 'master plan' was drawn up by London architect W G Habershon.[37] Yet none of these plans went forward, and even today they make their absence felt in the belt of open land or 20th century housing close to the town centre, comprising (clockwise from south) the Springwood Hall Gardens estate, Greenhead Park, more modern housing at the top of Trinity St and around Cedar Avenue, Edgerton Cemetery, Highfields allotments and St John's, Birkby, interrupted only by the 'ribbon development' of New North Rd.

Part of the explanation for this was the Ramsden estate's inability or unwillingness to grant long leases. Instead they had traditionally offered 'tenancies at will', with no formal security of tenure, or at best 60-year leases renewable every 20. It took private Acts of 1859 and 1867 to introduce 99- and then 999-year leases. Between these years, when Edgerton's development was at its peak, "the Ramsden Estate only offered leasehold on 99 years, [while] builders sought land from other landowners who offered 999 year terms".[38]

However another factor was the quality of the land in the 'empty arc', which Hathorn may have over-estimated. Following a similar path was a soft bed coal seam, with 19th century pits at Cooper Wood (now within Greenhead Park), Snodley (Cedar Mount), Bay Hall and Clare Hill. This would have made the land challenging to build on and, at Springwood, the Ramsdens eventually cut their losses on residential development and ran a colliery themselves from 1862 to 1877.[39]

Where residential development did go forward, control of the building process through the terms of leases gave landlords the opportunity, like a modern planning authority, to shape neighbourhoods. Thus the Thornhills developed Hillhouse, and the Fentons Longroyd Bridge, very differently from Edgerton. In those areas terraced housing was built for artisans; in Edgerton the aim was to create a secluded and exclusively residential suburb – and of course anyone choosing to build there would want the assurance that those taking neighbouring plots would be similarly constrained.

When the Thornhill trustees let a plot, therefore, they required a villa to be erected within 12 months, in line with the "plan elevation dimensions materials and workmanship" specified in a plan deposited with the trustees.[40] Before long a minimum building cost was also specified, to reinforce the message that only the best would do. The houses were to be insured for three-fourths of their value, rebuilt within a year if destroyed, and consent was required for any alterations. Initially no non-residential uses were permitted, although a later version allowed permission to be granted for "offensive trades".[41] The Lockwood leases give a sense of what these might be, explicitly precluding use of the properties by a "blacksmith, farrier, tanner, skinner, chymist, butcher or beerhouse-keeper or as and for an inn alehouse or victualling house" and prohibiting steam or fire engines; making of pots or pipes; burning of wood; making of glue, sizing, soap or candles; or "any other noisome, dangerous or offensive trade calling or business".[42] Similar conditions were imposed by the Fentons.[43]

The setting of the houses was also important. Villas on Lockwood and Varley land were essentially laid out along the main road, and there is no evidence that these smaller landlords played any role in planning the layout, but the Thornhill and Fenton trustees certainly did.

In the Thornhill case, road and plot layouts were in hand from the moment the 1852 Act was passed and there were evidently several versions. One which has survived, dated 27 February 1855 (fig.15), is substantially different from what came to pass. Drawn up by surveyor George Crowther and Kirkheaton landscape gardener W Pontey & Son, this bears the legend 'Plan of part of Miss Clara Thornhill's Estate in Lindley contiguous to Edgerton To be Let on Lease in Villa Sites for a Term of 999 Years'[44] – confirming that 'Edgerton' at that point was still seen as lying east of the Sunny Bank Beck. It shows a finer-grained street pattern, with more and smaller plots, than the eventual result. Presumably the estate had under-estimated the demand for the very large villa sites eventually achieved, many of them 4–5000 square yards.

Similarly, when the Thornhills acquired the adjoining 'Birkby' estate in 1858, Joshua Tolson's plan for 22 villas around a street grid was abandoned in favour of just eight particularly large plots, taking full advantage of the picturesque qualities identified by Tolson (see p.28) – at just the time that Varley quickly switched his plan from 13 plots to four as noted above (p.29). Many of the Thornhill road names had family roots – at Calverley (near Pudsey) they owned the manor and brought forward development proposals around the same time; Hungerford and Forester reflected Thornhill marriage partners; and Dingley was the Hungerford seat in Northamptonshire.[45] As to Kaffir Rd, Bryan and Henry Thornhill, nephews of Thomas Thornhill, had both recently served in the Eighth Kaffir War, which ended with the final defeat of the Ciskei Xhosa in February 1853.[46] (The name's survival through modern municipal politics is perhaps a surprise. Representations were made to Kirklees Council in 1982 for a change, by a South African resident, but rejected after consultation with neighbours.[47])

The estate took responsibility for laying out the roads and sewers – though this was recharged to the leaseholders. These works were completed by November 1854, by which time nearly £5000 had been spent on the three Thornhill developments at Edgerton, Lindley and Hillhouse.[48] The plot enclosed by Halifax Rd and Kaffir Rd was originally intended for a church, but in the meantime was reserved for the adjoining leaseholders, with ornamental trees to be planted. Tenders for landscaping were invited in November 1867 by two of the residents, Thomas Hirst of Willow Bank and James Burman of Woodbine (now Brantwood).[49] The church was never built, although when he died in 1875 Thomas Varley (see p.19) – already a benefactor of Lindley church – left £1000 for any committee proposing to provide one, as long as it was built within 20 years of his death.[50] By 1889 the scheme had evidently been abandoned and Edgerton Park comprised a bowling green, tennis courts and a small pavilion (fig.16), financed by private subscription and managed by a committee, presumably of the leaseholders.[51]

The Fenton trustees adopted much the same approach in the following decade. Their lay-out of substantial plots around Queen's Rd and Murray Rd, though adjusted in detail, is essentially what we see today, and they would go one better with two picturesquely curved triangular intersections.[52] Queen's Rd was a conventional mid-Victorian choice of name, while 'Murray' perhaps indicates that the litigious Eliza (see p.29) had been forgiven her sins.

Fig.15
Thornhill Estate sale map, 1855. Thornhill Rd, Hungerford Rd and Kaffir Rd (then Kaffir Place) are shown essentially as they would be built. But the link to the latter from the main road is Forester Rd; a curving version of Cleveland Rd appears as Calverley Place; and proposals for Dingley Grove (longer than today's Dingley Rd), Henry Terrace, Julia Place, Cleveland Parade and Vane Terrace all went unrealised.

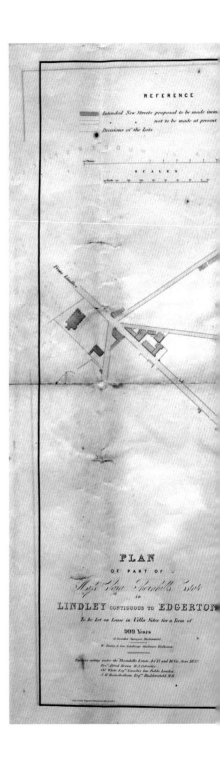

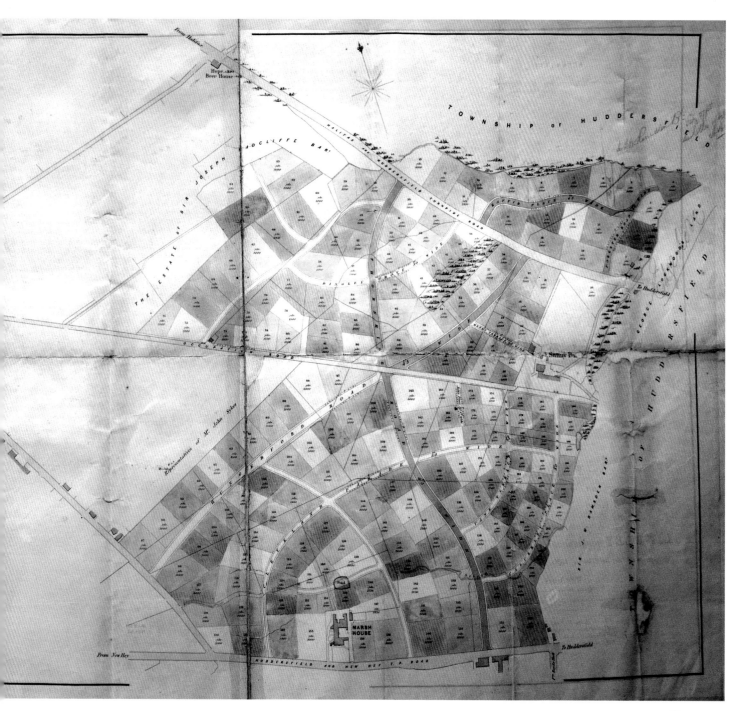

35

In most cases the leaseholder was also the occupier of the house. But some were built as investment properties and let out to tenants, whilst in other cases this would happen after the death of the original leaseholder. This enabled rather more social diversity among the residents than might have been the case if they had exclusively been owner-occupiers; and the creation of some modest homes alongside the grandest villas, particularly on the Lockwood and Fenton land, had the same effect. But the point should not be exaggerated: this was unequivocally a middle class suburb, and in the main an upper middle class one.

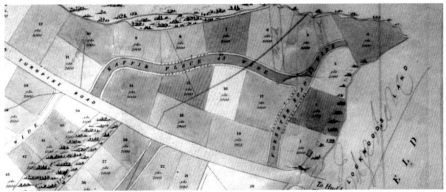

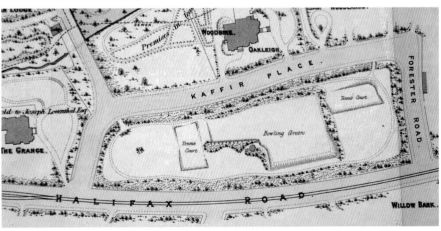

Fig.16
Edgerton Park in 1882 (bottom), compared with a detail from the 1855 Thornhill Plan (top).

The Built Character
of the Suburb

IN THE WORDS of the 2007 Conservation Area review report:

> The character of the Conservation Area is predominantly that of a leafy Victorian residential area, with large, architecturally interesting, detached buildings set in generous grounds. The mature trees, shrubs and hedges in the private gardens partially screen the buildings and create a sense of open space and area separated from the public highways by stone walls.[53]

The "architecturally interesting" buildings are in the full range of historicist styles available to Victorian architects, with neo-classical, Gothic and, from the 1860s, Italianate designs adopted in broadly equal measure. But while many of the houses can reasonably be labelled in these ways, others are too eclectic to categorise, if not as a whole then certainly in their wealth of detail. David Wyles cites the list description for Cleveland House, "one of the less elaborate mansions", which refers to Tuscan, Doric, Anglo-Saxon/Medieval and French features (see p.97).[54] Most are in hammer-dressed stone, though ashlar is often used for the classical houses. More than one might expect are semi-detached, but this is often disguised by setting two large semis at right-angles to each other, creating the illusion from most angles of a detached house.

For the first residents, the quality of the interiors was of course very important – and often no expense was spared to create an ambience appropriate to their social status. This is captured in the fine images, *overleaf*, of Oakwood in Hungerford Rd around the turn of the century, and its steep garden setting. (For more about Oakwood, see p.105.)

Fig.17 (overleaf)
Eight Oakwood (Hungerford Rd) photographs from an undated Freeman family album of around 1900.

As the conservation report notes, it is the placing of most of the houses in "generous grounds", and their leafy environment, which create the area's distinctive character. In these ways, Edgerton embodies mid-Victorian themes of privacy, seclusion and the separation of a female-centred domestic life from the male-dominated world of business and public affairs. In the case of the larger houses, this retreat from the world is emphasised by the provision – sometimes as later additions – of discreetly curving drives and lodges at the entrance, occupied by domestic or garden staff acting literally as 'gatekeepers' to the private world inside. As the urban historian Donald Olsen put it:

> The most successful suburb was the one that possessed the highest concentration of anti-urban qualities: solitude, dullness, uniformity, social homogeneity, barely adequate public transportation ... remoteness, both physical and psychological, from what is mistakenly regarded as the Real World.[55]

The landscape setting is relentlessly emphasised in the naming of the houses. The Sunny Bank glen which carved through the area gave rise to Glen View, Glenside and Glenwood, and several houses refer to banks in their names. But it is the wooded character which dominates – no fewer than seven house names draw on the oak, and three each on the elm, the ash and the holly, with beech, cedar, laurel, may and willow also putting in an appearance, alongside other plants such as sedge and fern.

Within this woodland setting, much effort went into the design and maintenance of the gardens (though the designers are unknown). Edgerton typified the garden philosophy summarised thus by the social historians Leonora Davidoff and Catherine Hall:

> In both image and practice the garden setting of the villa proclaimed the values of privacy, order, taste and appreciation of nature in a controlled environment. Gardens were now seen as an extension of the home, a conceit enhanced by the introduction of glass doors ('French windows') opening from parlour or dining room. Smaller, non-utilitarian gardens surrounding a separate house became an integral part of the romantic, anti-urban individualism of the middle class.[56]

Fig.18
Private Edgerton – the drive of
The Knowle, Edgerton Rd.

All these themes are regularly expressed in the sale particulars when the houses come to market, of which this is a fine 1860 example:

Lunnclough Hall [see p.115] is a New and Elegant Mansion, beautifully situated at Edgerton, 'the Belgravia of Huddersfield', a convenient distance from the town; it is built upon an eminence, completely detached, and surrounded with scenery of an undulating character; the lawn extends to three fronts, and a magnificent belt of full grown oak, ash and elm trees, brings out the fine lines of the style in which the house is built ... It is approached from the Halifax Rd, the distance from which is 120 yards, thus getting clear of the dust, and numerous annoyances of the Highway. It is magnificently grand in all its proportions, inside as well as outside; and it is a proper residence for a Merchant Prince, who can retire from the busy hum and turmoil of active life into this his quiet home, nested amidst nature's choicest products......

Although the whole composition evinces unity of feeling, there is as much variety of feature as we ever remember to have seen introduced successfully in a villa; indeed, perhaps a greater variety of windows, gables and buttresses than could be introduced in a building of that size [4 recep, 8 bed] with good effect, were it not supported by the corresponding interest and variety of the trees around it, which are here in admirable keeping with the picturesque outlines of the edifice.[57]

The atmosphere was also well evoked by Thomas Armstrong in his fictional rendition of Edgerton in the 1880s as Moorheaton,

.... with its big mansions, gardens like miniature parks, and private roads; griffins, lions and eagles on the pillars of entrances; domestics who would scorn service with less than two-carriage employers; and belfries on every block of stabling; of gardener's cottages at every main gate; and of the intrusion of rival gangs of labourers who shovelled heroically that their employer might not lag behind in proclaiming ownership of a lawn-tennis court.[58]

Fig.19
Powerful Edgerton – the tower of Lunnclough Hall, Kaffir Rd.

Architects

IN THE CASE of Lunnclough Hall, built in 1855 in a Tudor Gothic style for the chemical industry pioneer Read Holliday, the architect is identified on the plans as Pritchett & Sons. James Pigott Pritchett of York (1789–1868) was the distinguished architect of the Parish Church, Railway Station and Huddersfield College (also a Tudor Gothic building) and may well have designed Lunnclough Hall, though the firm maintained a Huddersfield office in which Pritchett's sons James and Charles worked in the 1840s and 1850s. Generally speaking, however, the original architects are frustratingly hard to identify. Plans submitted to the Corporation after 1868 are available, with some gaps, but by then most of the villas were built.

Before that, plans were submitted to the Thornhill estate but these have sadly been lost in recent years.[59] Moreover Huddersfield architects were only beginning in this period to distinguish themselves from builders – a smaller town than Leeds offered less opportunity for the emergence of an architectural profession – so it is likely that many of the villas of the 1850s and 1860s were put up by men as likely to call themselves builders as architects.

For the pre-1868 period, however, architects' names do sometimes emerge from newspaper adverts for building tenders; some houses were built after 1868, particularly on the Fenton land; and many of the houses were enlarged, often by billiard rooms – a craze from the 1880s – or had coach houses, stables or lodges added, in later years. From these sources, many of the responsible architects can be identified.[60]

The biggest contribution almost certainly came from John Kirk & Sons, the leading local practice by the 1860s. Kirk himself (1817–86) was a joiner's son who followed the classic route from master builder to architect, and he and his three sons were practising in Huddersfield and Dewsbury by 1862. His identified Edgerton work includes Oak Lea in Regent Rd (1869), Cedar Grove in Bryan Rd (1869) and its lodge opposite (1876), and Bankfield/Springfield, Queen's Rd (1869), all in a straightforward Italianate style. The latter's Gothic neighbour, Sedgefield, is almost certainly Kirk's work

Fig.20
Architect John Kirk; oil painting by F A Philips, 1876.

too. However, much of his work remains unattributed – the firm invited tenders for a dozen Edgerton houses in 1861–4 alone, when the Thornhill development was at its height and upper Edgerton must have been one large building site. Kirk also made additions and alterations to several other houses.

William Cocking (1817–74), architect of Britannia Buildings in St George's Square and today's RBS bank in Market Place, was responsible for the Italianate Viso House in Sunnybank Rd and perhaps for Bremen House on Edgerton Rd. W H Crossland (c1834–1909), a local architect who was to build his national reputation with Rochdale Town Hall and Royal Holloway College in Surrey, designed Marsh Field and West Mount, Edgerton Grove Rd in 1868.

Also active in the 1860s was John Eastwood (1821/2–1891), primarily a spinner but also a part-time architect/builder. As well as putting up his own Gladstone Mill in Firth St, he was responsible for Laurel Bank, Hungerford Rd in 1864, and a more modest pair of houses in Murray Rd (now nos 5 and 8) in 1871. He was also appointed builder of a pair of neo-classical villas, Ashleigh and Trafford House, on Halifax Rd, in 1863, though the architect was Ralph Nicholson of Halifax (d.1889). Edward Wyndham Tarn (1827–1900), the first Huddersfield architect to achieve RIBA qualification, sought tenders for two Edgerton villas in 1862, perhaps Clyde House and Bankfield.

By the 1870s two other prominent local architects were active in Edgerton. Ben Stocks (1838–1911) was the son of a builder/stonemason who trained at the Mechanics' Institute (which offered drawing and design classes from 1842) and worked for Kirks from 1863–68 before forming his own practice. As Brian Haigh has written,

> ... no commission was too small to merit Ben Stocks' attention; in addition to board schools, whole streets of houses, Nonconformist chapels and Sunday schools, mills, foundries, hotels, shops and offices, his output included privies, wash kitchens, wooden sheds and cupboards.[61]

He completed Huddersfield Town Hall after the death of J H Abbey, and was responsible for several Board schools. No complete Edgerton house by Stocks has been identified, but his work includes additions to several.

Born in the same year as Stocks, Edward Hughes (1838–86), like W H Crossland before him, was a pupil of George Gilbert Scott's, and practised in Huddersfield from 1871. Huddersfield's first Fellow of the Royal Institute of Architects, he was responsible for two of the town's most-lamented lost Victorian buildings, the 'romantic Gothic' Market Hall of 1878–80 and the onion-domed free classical Huddersfield Banking Co of 1881–2; surviving fine buildings include the Albert Hotel and the University's Ramsden Building. In Edgerton he is represented by the Tudor Gothic Thorn Hill (1875), and he also made minor additions elsewhere.

Willie Cooper (1862–1920) was articled to Hughes and eventually took over his practice. Noted for the Drill Hall, in Edgerton he was responsible for Deveron House, Queen's Rd (1905) and added substantially to Lunnclough Hall in 1889–93 and to several other villas.

By the later 19th century, then, Huddersfield had developed a capable and versatile architectural profession. However Edgerton's early residents also looked beyond Huddersfield to engage architects from Bradford, Manchester and Hull. As the perambulation will identify, there are houses by Lockwood & Mawson and Thomas & Francis Healey, both notable Bradford practices, and Salomons & Steinthal of Manchester, while G Faulkner Armitage of Altrincham undertook a celebrated (but demolished) extension to Stoneleigh in 1889 and interiors elsewhere.

Edgerton Society

SO MUCH, IN outline, for the houses of Edgerton. But who were the first occupants, and how did the social life of the suburb develop?[62]

Manufacturers

EDGERTON IS OFTEN characterised as a mill-owners' suburb, and indeed every Italianate or Gothic tower is routinely said to have given its owner the opportunity to keep a distant eye on his workforce in the town below. Undoubtedly manufacturers were the largest single occupational group among the early residents. But merchants and professionals were also well-represented, as we shall see – and towers were usually just a design statement.

Among the manufacturers, a good place to start is with the Martin family, who came early to Edgerton with little to their name and, over half a century, would become almost certainly its wealthiest family. Patrick Martin came from Ireland as a young man and was living in Dock Street in 1841 – hardly a salubrious part of town – as a 'pattern drawer', or textile designer, for John Taylor & Sons of Newsome Mills. He leased a plot from George Lockwood in 1849, on the corner of the main road and Luther Place, where he built a small Gothic house, Ashfield (now Roseneath). By 1859 he was in partnership with Joseph Liddell, and in 1864 they bought Wellington Mills at Oakes from the previous owner, George Walker of Lindley, who had apparently got into financial difficulties.

Under the leadership of three generations of the Martin family, Martin & Sons at Wellington Mills pioneered the local manufacture of fancy worsteds and were Huddersfield's largest employer by 1910, with 1400 workers on a four-and-a-half acre site.[63] The great wealth of the business spilled over into far more ostentatious living than Patrick Martin's modest Ashfield. His sons Henry and Edwin joined the business as partners in 1875, and by 1884 Henry had bought the lease of Stoneleigh, Bryan Rd, arguably the most imposing of all the Edgerton houses (see p.126). He died in 1910 leaving £419,557, making him a multi-millionaire in today's values – and that would have counted only personal property, not including the value of the business.[64] Henry's eldest son Horace, next in line to the business, lived next door at Beechwood, Bryan Rd from about 1900.

Another great industrial dynasty were the Armitages. The manufacturing business of Joseph Armitage & Sons had been established at Milnsbridge in 1822, and Joseph's own home was at Milnsbridge House. Where Patrick Martin was a 'self-made man', Armitage (pictured p.50) started out with landed wealth behind him, from estates at Honley. He had six sons and nine daughters, and the family proliferates through 19th century Huddersfield history. His eldest son George bought Edgerton Hill by 1839 – "in time", as John Brook puts it, "to witness the real development of Edgerton and to preside as probably the senior family in the district for the next sixty years or so". Succeeding his father as chairman of the firm, he returned to Milnsbridge when Joseph retired to Birkby Lodge in 1854, and was succeeded at Edgerton Hill by a younger brother, Edward, a substantial landowner with 73 acres in the 1873 survey. He and his son Alfred, who succeeded him at Edgerton Hill, were responsible for the development of adjoining Glebe St with terraced housing, on land bought from the Ramsden estate in 1892. Another brother, Captain Joseph Taylor Armitage, lived at Birkby Grange, and his son Charles Ingram Armitage came to live at Woodleigh, Bryan Rd after his marriage in 1877; whilst another of George's sons, Joseph Armitage Armitage (sic), a property developer, was at Wood Field, Queen's Rd, around 1880 before moving to Storthes Hall near Kirkburton.[65]

Joseph Armitage senior was a great public figure of late Georgian and early Victorian Huddersfield, and his sons and grandsons followed suit. George succeeded him as chairman of the magistrates' bench, and J T and J A Armitage were JPs too. George was also a founding vice-president of the

Fig.21
Worsted manufacturer Henry Martin of Stoneleigh, Bryan Rd.

Chamber of Commerce in 1853 and a director of the Huddersfield Banking Co, while Edward was vice-president of the technical college in the 1880s. This combination of private and public roles was a common pattern for Edgerton's leading men.

There were another dozen woollen manufacturers among the original occupants, and they would soon be followed by famous millowner names such as Crosland and Crowther. But other industries were represented too. Henry Martin was the third owner of Stoneleigh, which was built for the cigar manufacturer Edward Beaumont in 1861, though soon sold to woollen manufacturer Samuel Turner Learoyd. Another Learoyd, Frederick, who branched out from the same family to become a cotton spinner, was the first owner of Oakleigh in Kaffir Rd, while Edward Brooke, who established the tile and firebrick works at Fieldhouse off Leeds Rd, was responsible for Oakley House, at the corner of Halifax and Hungerford Roads.

Another manufacturer who had a major impact on Huddersfield's industrial history, and on Edgerton, was Read Holliday. Rising like Patrick Martin from humble origins, in 1830 he founded his business converting gasworks by-products to chemical agents for the textile industry. This was the modest start of what became a major dyestuffs producer at Turnbridge and eventually, in the 20th century, one of the tributary streams that flowed into ICI at Bradley. Holliday took one of the first Thornhill leases, in 1854, for a plot off the NE corner of Kaffir Rd (then Forrester Place), where Lunnclough Hall was built on the secluded and picturesque site glowingly described above (p.41). In the 1860s he turned to property development as a hobby, commissioning three more villas in Kaffir Rd – Woodlands, Hollinhurst and Holmwood – before retiring to Harrogate in the 1870s, where he built several more.

By then Read Holliday was the very model of a bourgeois gentleman, but in his younger days he had been a political radical – a supporter of the republican atheist Richard Carlile and subsequently a trustee of the Hall of Science in Bath Street, established in 1838 as the meeting place of the town's Owenite Socialists.[66] If the combination of political radicalism, industrial entrepreneurship and housebuilding seems exotic, Edgerton surprisingly offers another example of the same combination in George Brook and his son, also George, whose story is set out below (pp.136–7).

Merchant princes

BEFORE IT WAS a mill town Huddersfield was a commercial centre, with wealthy merchants buying and supplying wool to the clothiers of the surrounding villages and gathering in the finished cloth for sale at home and abroad. This commercial heritage was reflected in the development of the town centre, from the opening of the Cloth Hall in 1766 to the great warehouses and showrooms of the Victorian 'new town' a century later, and the town's leading public figures in the first half of the 19th century were more often merchants and landowners than manufacturers.[67] Naturally this accumulation of wealth found expression in Edgerton, with wool merchants almost equalling the woollen manufacturers amongst the first residents (and of course merchants and manufacturers were not mutually exclusive).

Some of the most notable merchants were concentrated along a short stretch of Halifax Rd from Cleveland Rd to Thornhill Rd – Thomas Hirst at Willow Bank, Wright Mellor at Cote Royd, George Barker at Ashleigh, Edward Woodhead at Trafford House and Joseph Lowenthal at The Grange. The latter was one of a substantial German contingent – eastern Germany had become a major source of fleeces by this time, as the woollen industry expanded beyond what local sources could supply and domestic sheep-breeding gave priority to meat over wool. Those who came to Edgerton, as well as Lowenthal, included Henry Fischer at The Knowle; his partner Edward Huth of Oakfield Lodge; Maximilian Liebmann of Cleveland House (originally Berlin House); James Liebreich, of Edgerton Lodge and then Bankfield (Edgerton Rd); Henry Anders, of The Mount and then Thornleigh; and the Zossenheim brothers, Maximilian and Julius, shipping agents at Clyde House and Edgerton Bank respectively.

Nor were these migrations entirely one way. In an earlier generation Joseph Brook of Greenhead had built his business on the import of German

Fig.22
Wool merchant Joseph Lowenthal of The Grange, Halifax Rd.

wool and his sons George Henry and Richard joined the business. Richard Brook moved to Berlin in the 1840s, marrying into a wealthy Berlin banking family, while George Henry lived at Edgerton Lodge until a business crash in 1852 led him to 'downsize' to Edgerton Cottage.[68] Whilst Huddersfield had nothing to equal Bradford's 'Little Germany' quarter, all these men represented a substantial trading and cultural relationship with Germany, with which Britain was closely linked, from the Royal Family downwards, until the calamity of the First World War.

Professionals and tradesmen

ALONGSIDE THE MANUFACTURERS and merchants were to be found a contingent of what would now be called 'white collar' professionals. Amongst these the largest single group were the lawyers, who were much in demand to support the town's commercial culture. John Freeman, practising from around 1835, was prominent among these. He lived first at Edgerton Bank before having the very substantial Oakwood (Hungerford Rd) built in 1863 (see pp.38–39, 105). His partner Thomas Brook built Woodleigh (Bryan Rd) around the same time, moving there from the Croft House in Marsh. Their later partner, Joseph Batley, became the first Town Clerk when the Borough was incorporated in 1868.

Much legal work derived from the complexity of property transactions as the town's development forged ahead. For the same reason the land agents were a significant professional group. George Henry Crowther, who worked for the Thornhill, Fenton and other local estates, moved from Fixby to Thorn Hill, newly built in about 1875. His counterpart Thomas Brook, who worked mainly for the Ramsden estate (and not to be confused with his legal namesake just mentioned), was at Mayfield from about 1864, while the lengthy tenancy at Edgerton House of Ramsden estate clerk Isaac Hordern was noted above (p.20). Woodville on Edgerton Rd was built by another Thornhill agent, Frederick Holroyd, though for letting out rather than his own occupation. Nearby at Edgerton Cottage, the long-term occupants from 1852 into the 20th century were the insurance agent George Henry Brook and his son George Smith Brook, an actuary.

A modest number of retail 'tradesmen' were also among the first occupants of Edgerton. The Market St boot and shoe makers Henry and John Liddell built the two houses known as The Mount in 1851/2, with Henry occupying one of them until his death in 1866. The ironmonger Ludlam Ramsden had a house in Murray Rd, while the King St chemist and druggist Robert Fell built Somerville (Hungerford Rd) in about 1863 and lived there until 1910. But the largest group among the retailers were the linen drapers – Frederick Hudson who built Edgerton Hill, Robert Owen who built Edgerton Villa and John William Walker who put up Burleigh and Elm Lea (now Elm Crest) on Queen's Rd.

There was also a small contingent of what might now be seen as 'intellectuals'. The portrait painter and musician Samuel Howell was the first owner of Brooklyn, now Bryan Wood (Bryan Rd) in 1863. The architect James Radcliffe built The Knowle on Edgerton Rd, though again not for his own use, while the bookseller Joseph Brook – another Improvement Commissioner[69] – came to live across the road at Glenwood in 1863 after the death of its first owner. But many of Edgerton's industrial and commercial residents, as will be shown below, had extensive cultural interests and artistic collections; to be a businessman in a Northern manufacturing town was by no means necessarily to be a philistine.[70]

Public and private life

MANY OF THE MALE heads of Edgerton's early households were also heavily involved in the public life of the town, which developed apace from mid-century. For example, of 102 men who served as Huddersfield Improvement Commissioners between 1848 and 1868, at least 21 lived in Edgerton, which barely existed at the start of the period; if the focus is narrowed to those serving after 1855, the proportion rises to 17 out of 74. In the same period a good many Edgerton figures were to be found

Fig.23
Joseph Armitage (of Milnsbridge House), portrayed by Samuel Howell of Bryan Wood, Bryan Rd.

serving as Waterworks Commissioners or Infirmary Governors – though only one sat, for one year, on the directly-elected and more plebeian Board of [poor law] Guardians. Similarly, in the period after the establishment of the Corporation in 1868, the Borough magistrates' bench in 1870 and the School Board in 1871, many Edgerton gentlemen served on these new bodies, and as county magistrates.

The Corporation was contested between Tories and Liberals, while the main cleavage on the School Board was between Church (Anglican) and 'undenominational' (essentially Non-Conformist) candidates. All these allegiances were well-represented in the households of Victorian Edgerton. Sundays would find the families assembled for worship at the Parish Church, Holy Trinity, St Stephen's Lindley or St Thomas's, Longroyd Bridge; at Highfields and Brunswick St Congregationalist Chapels; and by the end of the century at Lindley or Gledholt Methodist Church.

Public life was overwhelmingly male, with Marion Huth's membership of the School Board (see p.125) a rare exception. Nor were Edgerton women gainfully employed outside the home – a survey of 77 households in the 1891 Census found no employed wives and only two daughters with jobs (a school proprietor and a teacher).[71] But within the home, as social historians of the period have emphasised, the wives ruled. They were mothers of large families – up to ten children being not uncommon – and managers of the household servants. As Mrs Beeton put it, in the opening sentence of her *Household Management* (1861),

> As with the COMMANDER OF AN ARMY, or the leader of any enterprise, so it is with the mistress of the house.

In her social history of the Victorian home, however, Judith Flanders argues that Beeton's and other manuals preached an upper middle class ideal actually out of reach of most suburban households.[72] Confirming this, Kathleen Brown's analysis of Edgerton in 1891 shows that typical establishments were not large. Although Stoneleigh had nine indoor servants (fig.24), and Ravensdeane seven, the most common number was three (27 households out of 78), with two staff in 20 of the households

and just one in 12. (However lodges were omitted from the analysis and gardeners, coachmen and other outdoor servants therefore not represented.) The need to accommodate the servants is reflected in the lodges, cottages, service wings and attics of many of the larger villas.

Flanders also emphasises just how much the servants and their 'commander' had to attend to. These houses had many rooms, each with its proper functions; domestic equipment was in its infancy, with few 'mod cons'; and in furniture and fittings, the fashion of the day was of course for what modern taste would regard as a great deal of 'clutter' – ornamenting the interiors, speaking to the owner's wealth and social status, but also gathering a great deal of dust. The rich profusion of objects in the typical Edgerton home is brought to life from time to time when a house clearance brings the contents into view at a public sale (fig.25).

Fig.24
The domestic staff of Stoneleigh, Bryan Rd in the late 19th century.

Houses often grew larger over time, to reflect the growing prosperity, families and establishments of their occupiers, whose recreational pursuits often centred on the home. At least a dozen billiard rooms were added to Edgerton houses from 1870 onwards, with a particular concentration in the 1880s and 1890s – it was a late Victorian craze, and the English Billiard Association was founded in 1885.[73] A slightly later development was the addition of conservatories and greenhouses – the Huddersfield Floral & Horticultural Society was re-established in 1906, with Edgerton's Edward Booth Woodhead (see p.108) playing a leading role. Gardens could form

Fig.25
Sale of contents of Woodbine, Kaffir Rd (later Brantwood), 1879.

WOODBINE, UPPER EDGERTON PARK, HUDDERSFIELD.

On Wednesday, 24th, and Thursday, 25th September, 1879.

EDDISON AND TAYLOR have received instructions from James Burman, Esq., who is leaving the town, to SELL BY AUCTION, on Wednesday and Thursday, September 24th and 25th, all the elegant and costly FURNISHINGS, pictures, richly cut glass, china, bronzes, electro-plate, and the numerous ornamental articles contained in the above-named residence.

In the Reception Rooms are a SUITE OF SEVEN DISSIMILAR CHAIRS, couch and reclining chairs, upholstered in blue rep, with double set of extra covers complete; a richly carved 5ft. 6in. CHEFFONIER, having shaped marble top and mirror, paneled doors surmounted by a high circular top mirror, enclosed in handsomely designed frame.

The above are all of the choicest Italian Walnut Wood, and are specimens of the best workmanship. A massive DINING ROOM SUITE in Spanish mahogany, including chairs, easy chairs, and couch, in maroon morocco leather. DINING TABLE, with extension leaves to 9 feet. Handsome mahogany 7ft. SIDEBOARD, of splendid proportions, having a large British plate mirror back, encircled by a finely-executed framework of vine leaves and fruit. Handsome open BOOK-CASE, or Whatnot, 4ft. wide and 4ft. 6in. high, specially designed, having small drawers in the underparts. Magnificent CHIMNEY GLASSES, 72in. by 60in., and 78in. by 60in. respectively, superbly mounted in gilded frames. Sofa tables and ladies' work table in harmony with the other appointments. Ormolu mounted and other fenders, with fireirons and ashes pan to match; superior coal vases. Complete sets of window draperies in rep, rich lace curtains and deep fringe valances.

Best quality BRUSSELS CARPETS, as planned to the numerous apartments, large size wool skin hearthrugs and door mats.

In the ENTRANCE HALL are a HAT and UMBRELLA STAND, with mirror; pair of hall chairs and a side table, having marble slab, all en suite in light oak; barometer, butler's tray and stand. 8ft. bagatelle table and fittings, wide Brussels stairs carpets and heavy brass rods.

The PICTURES present several pleasing specimens in WATER COLOURS from the pencils of Sykes, Booth, McIntyre, and others; OIL PAINTINGS by Cooke, Garthwaite, Jones, McIntyre, Veevers, and other artists of merit; a fine proof engraving of Frith's fine picture, "The Railway Station;" several choice chromos and oleographs elegantly framed in gilt.

Amongst the ORNAMENTAL ITEMS are numerous bronzes in groups and figures, tall Dresden vases, fine parian busts and figures under glass shades, &c.

The Glass and China Closets contain an elegant assortment for the dinner, breakfast, and tea tables.

The Electro Plate is of the best quality.

The BEDROOM APPOINTMENTS comprise a costly SUITE in POLISHED BIRCH of rich figure, including a Tudor bedstead, with cornice and footboard of artistic design; a Winged WARDROBE, with plate-glass centre door; a pair of toilet tables, with cabriole supports, the washstand having marble top; a Duchesse toilet table, with 5ft. mirror and full complement of drawers and fittings; dressing chest, pedestal cupboard, commode, towel rail, set of chairs, upholstered seats, toilet services, window cornices in gilt, trimmed window draperies and bed hangings in blue rep; a SPANISH MAHOGANY TUDOR BEDSTEAD, hung with crimson damask; pair toilet tables, chests of mahogany drawers, large toilet glasses in mahogany frames, handsome cheval class in mahogany; patent spring, hair, wool, and other mattresses; feather beds, small painted Tudor bedstead and iron French bedstead, with mattresses and hangings, &c.

The DOMESTIC OFFICES are replete with requisite appliances for the kitchen and laundry, all in excellent condition.

Detailed Catalogues are in course of preparation, and may be had at the Auctioneers' Offices, 6, High-street, Huddersfield, five days prior to the sale.

The whole will be on view on Monday only, the 22nd September, 1879, to holders of catalogues, from 10-0 a.m. to 4-0 p.m.

Sale to commence each day at 11 o'clock.

53

the setting for fashionable parties. By the turn of the century it was common to call in an outside caterer, often Whiteleys in Westgate, to service these, perhaps serving a peach melba made from fruit grown in the house's conservatory. The area was also dotted with tennis courts. And no home was complete without its piano, where the family could gather to sing – perhaps in a dedicated music room if space allowed. Performances of two 'Edgerton Polkas', composed in 1870 and 1876, may have been part of the repertoire.[74]

Church attendance and home entertainment were two ways in which Edgerton families were strongly networked (as we might say today). The male heads of household would have encountered each other constantly in public and business life, and in the town's growing number of clubs and societies. Prestigious among them was the Borough Club, founded in 1879 and occupying handsome premises in Ramsden St, opposite the Town Hall. An Edgerton Cricket Club was established in 1863, "under the patronage of several of the most influential gentlemen of the town", and Beechwood in Bryan Rd even sported its own cricket team.[75] Their sons, meanwhile, created a carefully regulated social life – or, cynically, a marriage market – through the interesting institution of Bachelors' Balls. These took place, though not annually, at least from the 1860s to the 1890s, and were reported in the local press. A surviving minute book of the Ball committees in 1877 and 1881 gives a snapshot of the arrangements.[76] In 1877, 42 bachelors constituted the nucleus of the event, each entitled, for a subscription of five guineas (£5.25) to invite two ladies and one other gentleman, not a Huddersfield bachelor. The

Programme

Stoneleigh,   Jan. 7th,

Fig.26
Programme for a ball at
Stoneleigh, Bryan Rd on 7
January 1897.

ball commenced on Friday night, 20 April, with 'quadrilles at 8.30' and 20 or so dances to follow; a similar programme from Stoneleigh in 1897 is illustrated. Supper and wines were supplied by the George Hotel; the entertainment ended with 'carriages at 3 a.m.'; but luncheon was available at 1 pm on Saturday for those who had not tired of the company. Edgerton had a majority on the ten-man committee, with three Armitages (see p.46), two Lowenthals (p.48) and H S Brook (p.87).

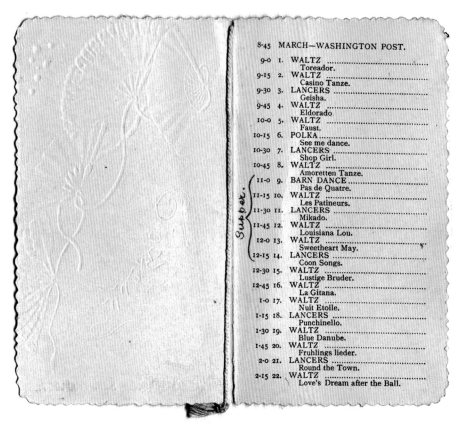

8·45 MARCH—WASHINGTON POST.

Time	No.	Dance	Title
9·0	1.	WALTZ	Toreador.
9·15	2.	WALTZ	Casino Tanze.
9·30	3.	LANCERS	Geisha.
9·45	4.	WALTZ	Eldorado
10·0	5.	WALTZ	Faust.
10·15	6.	POLKA	See me dance.
10·30	7.	LANCERS	Shop Girl.
10·45	8.	WALTZ	Amoretten Tanze.
11·0	9.	BARN DANCE	Pas de Quatre.
11·15	10.	WALTZ	Les Patineurs.
11·30	11.	LANCERS	Mikado.
11·45	12.	WALTZ	Louisiana Lou.
12·0	13.	WALTZ	Sweetheart May.
12·15	14.	LANCERS	Coon Songs.
12·30	15.	WALTZ	Lustige Bruder.
12·45	16.	WALTZ	La Gitana.
1·0	17.	WALTZ	Nuit Etoile.
1·15	18.	LANCERS	Punchinello.
1·30	19.	WALTZ	Blue Danube.
1·45	20.	WALTZ	Fruhlings lieder.
2·0	21.	LANCERS	Round the Town.
2·15	22.	WALTZ	Love's Dream after the Ball.

Supper.

Whether or not as a direct result of these occasions, marriages between young Edgerton neighbours were not infrequent. Newly-formed couples would then need a home of their own to start building a family. Although some families stayed put for decades, usually where the long-leaseholder was also the occupier, other houses, sub-let to tenants, saw quite frequent turnover. There was also a good deal of movement in and out of Edgerton as careers and families waxed and waned. There is a consistent pattern of upward mobility – both socially and often topographically too. As the perambulation below will illustrate, families often arrived in Edgerton from more modest houses lower down the town's westerly slopes, in the Newhouse/Highfields/New North Rd area (see p.23). There was also a good deal of movement within the suburb, between the varied house sizes it had to offer. In fewer cases, and later in life, there might be a further 'upward move' by successful families to one of the 'villa mansions' further out, such as High Royd (Honley) or Storthes Hall; or indeed to a grander house in North Yorkshire – George Armitage moved to Nunthorpe Hall near Middlesbrough – or to the coast.

All of this reflected the considerable prosperity of most Edgerton lives. A glimpse of the fortunes to be made is provided by probate data. Looking at a sample of ten Edgerton wills proved from 1892 to 1923, Kathleen Brown found personal wealth ranging from Benjamin Halstead's £5,592 in 1896 to Henry Martin's £419,557 in 1910.[77] Before the wills were read and proved, however, the passing of an Edgerton gentleman was usually marked by a large public funeral – with the lists of those in attendance testifying again to the highly networked nature of this society – and extensive obituaries in the local press. And his final resting place, of course, was often in Edgerton Cemetery.

Fig.27
Illustrated here is the Cleveland House reception of the 27 July 1904 wedding of Edith Hopkinson to Arthur, son of J E Walker of New North House, with about 230 guests attending. Mr J E Ibeson's band played selections during the afternoon.

L E Y

MBY Y

Birkby

BM 4

Daisy Lee

Spaniel Royd

Rose Hill

Birkby Hall

Birkby Brewery

Bay Hall Common

Birkby Fold
Holroyds Alms Houses

Birkby Lodge

Wheat House

Spring Place

DISTRICT

Lee Head
Spink Nest Inn

Union
Workhouse

Bay Hall

Edgerton

Sunny Bank

Edgerton Villa
Edgerton Cottage

Blacker
Lane
Wood

BOUNDARY

Woodfield Cottage

Edgerton Hill

Croft House

MARSH

Edgerton Ho.
Edgerton

Marsh House

Edgerton Lodge

Snod

High field

IMPROVEMENT

Hollin Carr

Marsh House Inn

Marsh Fold

Marsh

M a r s h

PittsWood

West Field Terrace

Trinity Church

Dike End

York House

M A R S H

LOCAL BOARD

Marsh Mill

Luck Lane End Hill

GREAT HEAD

TOWNSHIP

Black Rock
Heaton Fold

Fish Pond

Head Lane

HUDDERSFIELD

HUD

Quakers Row

DISTRICT

Water Works

Completing the Suburb

EDGERTON'S SECLUSION AND domestic privacy have been constant themes as we have described the suburb's development. As a wider study of Huddersfield's suburbs noted, while most of them developed with local facilities:

> Edgerton in a way comes nearer to the modern suburb in its lack of amenities. Here general access to private transport enabled its inhabitants to consider Huddersfield, a mile away, still to be their shopping and social centre. For this wealthy enclave the horse and carriage acted in the same way as the motor car today.[78]

And to this day, the area remains devoid of shops, pubs and public buildings. But even the most private of developments is dependent on public infrastructure and subject to public regulation.

The public domain

IN 1868, HUDDERSFIELD's belated incorporation as a borough brought Edgerton within its purview. The new Corporation had several precursors. Although, as noted above, many Edgerton men were Huddersfield Improvement Commissioners, that body's writ ran only 1200 yards from the Market Place. Two of their milestone-like boundary markers, inscribed 'HIB 1848', can still be seen at the brow of the hill on Trinity St and New North Rd (fig.29). None of Edgerton was within their domain.

Until 1860, the centuries-old parochial authorities of Marsh hamlet (one of five making up Huddersfield township) and Lindley-cum-Quarmby township were the only local government bodies covering Edgerton. (The boundaries are not quite what one would expect from today's mental maps, with most land north of the main road, including the Cemetery, Queen's Rd and Bryan Rd areas, falling into Marsh – see fig.28.) In that year Lindley took advantage of the 1858 Public Health Act, which offered regulatory powers over highways, drainage and nuisances, to constitute a Local Board for its area, and Marsh followed suit in 1861; both lasted only until Huddersfield's incorporation in 1868, and only a couple of Edgerton gentlemen played any part as members.

During its short life the Lindley Board was quite vigorous and professional in its endeavours to improve the area's basic amenities.[79] Chaired for several years by Lindley industrialist James Nield Sykes, from the outset it employed a part-time surveyor. Within months it was negotiating with the Thornhill estate to take over the sewers and to adopt some estate roads as public streets. It provided 'causeways' (pavements) along the turnpike road and other roads retained by the estate, and enforced repair obligations on the Thornhill lessees. It covered some of the watercourses cutting through the area. Spurred by deputations of residents, it pursued gas and mains water supply for the area. The town's water supply at the time was managed by the Huddersfield Waterworks Commissioners (HWC), a quasi-public body, and in 1866 Lindley Board supported legislation to extend the HWC's permitted boundaries. Gas was provided by private companies: sites for 22 gas lamps were determined in 1865, after a residents' deputation, and a tender for supply by Huddersfield Gas Co accepted in 1866. In the same year the Board began to require the submission for its approval of building plans. In 1867 it pursued the repeal of the Halifax and Huddersfield Turnpike Act and the removal of its tollgates; the one at Edgerton Bar (Blacker Lane) was indeed removed that year, when the turnpike trustees sold it to the Ramsden estate, probably for the stone.[80] But the Board also supported Lindley's incorporation into the new borough, and ended without ceremony on 2 September 1868.

The Marsh Local Board was a much less impressive body.[81] At its second meeting, on 17 April 1861, its minutes record "Nothing to do particular and

Fig.29
The boundary stone of the Huddersfield Improvement Commissioners' jurisdiction, still in place at the top of New North Rd.

only 6 [of 9] members present". Meetings with "no business to transact" followed quite frequently, and it was perhaps a ratepayer protest that occasioned the following curious motion in June 1864:

> ...for the future all money received for sand and spent on beverages shall be discontinued, and such money has perfectly [sic] known by the ratepayers as sand brass shall be appropriated for the benefit of this Hamlet and entered in the books in a similar way as rates.

At the end of 1866 the minutes record, more formally and in much improved handwriting, a turn towards professionalism.[82] By April 1867 officers were appointed and bye-laws adopted; in June tenders were invited for 80 gas lamps (installed by October); and in July the first building plan was approved. At this point the Board wanted to stay in business, resolving unlike Lindley to oppose the incorporation Bill by all legitimate means, "not seeing any advantages to this district to be derived from such incorporation". But the decision was later reversed and Marsh Local Board passed away, again without ceremony, on 20 September 1868.

The new Huddersfield Corporation, instituted a generation after some of its neighbours, was soon making up for lost time with a pioneering programme of municipal enterprise. The waterworks undertaking was acquired in 1869 and new reservoirs put in hand to meet the town's growing needs, while the Gas Co was acquired in 1871. Plans were required from the outset for all building work – providing the rich archival trove which continues to inform the town's architectural history. And in 1883 Huddersfield was the first town to initiate municipal steam tramways. The service to Edgerton (Bryan Rd) via New North Rd commenced on 12 January 1884, extended to Lindley via Holly Bank Rd on 11 October 1886, and the splendidly restored shelter at the top of Clayton Fields is the visible legacy today; before then, there may have been a private horse bus service. Electric trams replaced steam on 14 February 1901, and from 1911 the Holly Bank Rd service was dropped and the main line extended to Birchencliffe (and eventually to West Vale).[83]

Other elements of modern 'infrastructure' were also reaching Edgerton from the 1860s. A Royal Mail pillar box was provided on the main road

Fig.30
The West Vale tram arriving in Westgate from Edgerton.

outside Glenside in June 1862 (London had the first in the country in 1855). Gas street lighting was appearing, as noted above, from the late 1860s. In 1887 the National Telephone Co sought permission to erect three telephone poles on Halifax Rd, and in June 1890 the *Huddersfield Chronicle* reported that William Shaw at Bremen House, Edgerton Rd was able to secure quick attention to a house fire in Imperial Rd, as he "has telephone communication between his home and the exchange" – evidently still a novelty at that date, a dozen or so years after the first lines in London.[84] In 1893 the Corporation opened its own electricity generating station, near the gas works on Leeds Rd, and in Bryan Rd Charles Mills of Thornleigh acquired a connection in 1894.[85]

Changes in the housing market

MUCH OF THE DEVELOPMENT of denser semi-detached and terraced housing to the south of the main road, along Imperial, Cleveland and Thornhill Roads, dates from the 1880s and 1890s, when the borough's population was growing rapidly. The landowners were the Thornhill, Lockwood and Ramsden estates. These roads are largely included in the Edgerton Conservation Area, in what are now defined as Character Areas 3–5, as distinct from the 'core Edgerton' – Character Area 1 – which is the focus of this study. Although there is much good quality housing, the urban grain is quite different; most of it would be seen as Marsh rather than Edgerton; and any analysis would over-extend this publication.

As the mid-century economic transformation of the town slowed, however, and family sizes began to fall, it became increasingly difficult for landowners to market land for more spacious villa development. In 1882 a substantial area of freehold building land north of Bryan Rd, in the Reap Hirst area, failed to find a buyer.[86] Then, in 1896, Joseph Fox (of Daisy Lea, Lindley) brought to auction a large part of the Norwood estate, on the north side of Halifax Rd from Banney Royd (not yet built – see p.66) to Birkby Rd – essentially the area of today's housing estates at Inglewood Avenue and Norwood Park. Like the Thornhill and Fenton releases of mid-century, this was a serious attempt to market 18 acres of land for villa development, with the sale plan detailing five proposed roads – but again there were no takers.[87]

By this time the original developers had no further opportunities in Edgerton, even had the market permitted, and indeed began to reduce their commitments. The Thornhill estate sold the freeholds of the Bryan Rd houses to their occupiers or to investors for the ground rents, the last of them in March 1889.[88] By then the Fenton estate had adopted a more comprehensive disposal policy.

The trustees at their annual meeting in December 1884 received notice of the death of Miss Mary Fenton, the tenant for life, "and consequent arrival of the time of distribution and division amongst the several parties entitled in reversion to the Fenton Estates etc". The sigh of relief as their management responsibilities come to an end is almost audible; the agents are instructed to dispose of all freehold property and to assign the leasehold ground rents amongst seven beneficiaries, and the trustees' last meeting is held in January 1886. The Lockwood trustees remained in possession of their land until 1934 but then, shortly after the death of George Lockwood's last surviving son, sold out to Lady Kaye, formerly of Norwood (see below) and by then resident in Surrey.[89] But the Thornhill estate remains very much in business today, and continues to collect the ground rents from much of Edgerton.[90]

Fin-de-siecle opulence

THE CLASSIC DEVELOPMENT of villas on 1–2 acre sites, then, seemed exhausted by about 1890, with the energies of developers going into the denser housing south of the main road towards Marsh. But the Norwood estate was developed at this time, in a grander manner than anything yet seen in Edgerton. By the time Joseph Fox brought much of it to market in 1896, he had already released a plot at the Birkby Rd end, where the Lindley

THE BUILDING NEWS, SEPT 12, 1902.

NORWOOD HUDDERSFIELD · J HATCHARD SMITH FRIBA ARCT

Fig.31
The lost mansion of Norwood,
demolished in 1959.

Fig.32
Upper Edgerton's 'triangle of opulence' in 1905. (Reproduced here from the Ordnance Survey at approx. 1:6500.)

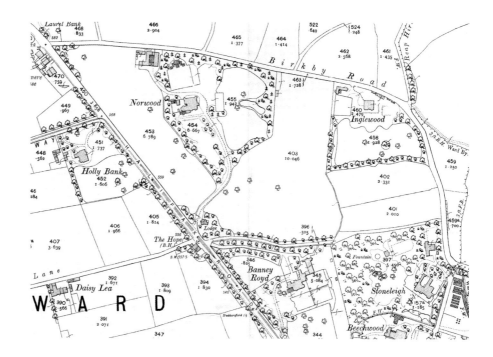

manufacturer Arthur Walker commissioned a substantial villa, **Norwood**, from John Kirk & Sons in 1891, in an elaborate classical style but not particularly large. Walker's business struggled, however, and by 1901 he had 'downsized' to a more modest house in Sunnybank Rd.

Norwood was bought from Walker by Joseph Henry Kaye of Hazelgrove, Edgerton Rd, another manufacturer, whose upward mobility contrasted with Walker's descent. Kaye bought Fox's unsold land from the 1896 offer and, in 1899–1901, had Kirk's villa enlarged and remodelled, with a striking three-storey octagonal tower topped by a steep turret roof, and a baronial hall among 17 rooms within. Architecturally this was quite a concoction: "The details seem to be mostly based on Elizabethan models, but the porch has what may be Gothic buttresses and an Italian Renaissance-looking semi-circular hood, and perhaps the octagonal tower owes something to

French chateaux."[91] The attribution in the architectural press is to country house architect John Hatchard Smith, but the plans are signed by Abbey & Hanson of Huddersfield. It seems they may have been prepared "under the superintendence" of Smith, who may have undertaken the interior of the new hall.[92] It was surrounded by 12 acres of beautiful gardens.

J H Kaye was a worsted manufacturer (of Kaye & Stewart, Lockwood); a businessman of national stature, as director of the Lancs & Yorks Railway, the LNWR and eventually the LMS, and of Lloyds Bank; and a local public figure, among other things a founder of the World War I hospital at Royds Hall. In the early 1920s, Norwood Grange was added at the east end of the enlarged plot, for Joseph and his wife (soon his widow: he died unexpectedly in 1923), while his son Henry took on Norwood. Norwood Grange was bought in the early 1930s by the parents of James (later Lord) Hanson, the swashbuckling businessman of the Thatcher era, and survives today, entirely surrounded by more recent housing. But the big house, Norwood, also bought by Robert Hanson in 1938, was demolished in 1959. The Inglewood Avenue development of superior modern homes, which occupies the site, retained ponds from the gardens and recycled some of Norwood's stone,[93] while the house's fine boundary wall also survives along Halifax Rd and Birkby Hall Rd.

At the same time as Norwood was being enlarged, the accountant W H Armitage commissioned **Banney Royd** (listed grade I), the house he had commissioned from "that remarkable Manchester architect" Edgar Wood,[94] on an adjacent 7-acre plot to the south, also sold by Joseph Fox. Wood's mother was one of the Sykes clan of Lindley, and his link to that prosperous manufacturing family led him to a series of Huddersfield commissions – he was working on Lindley Clock Tower at the same time as Banney Royd. The house is very different in style from Norwood – a Jacobean Pennine hall house inflected by Art Nouveau influences and details – but, with five principal rooms and eight bedrooms on a seven-acre site, shared with it a scale rarely seen in Victorian Edgerton.[95]

On its east side, Banney Royd is bordered by the similarly-sized plot of Stoneleigh; and beyond that lies Rose Hill. These are earlier houses but

Fig.33
Art nouveau detail of Banney Royd's dining room fireplace.

Fig.34
Banney Royd, Halifax Rd.

underwent major changes in the late C19 and early C20 to rival the splendour of Norwood and Banney Royd; they are included in the perambulation (pp.126–32).

On the triangle of land (fig.32) where Edgerton, Lindley and Birkby meet, then, the suburban villa tradition gave way in the 1890s to something rather grander.[96] These turn-of-the-century developments were written up in leading architectural journals, and the occupiers also rose above the ranks of even Edgerton's upper middle class. Ernest Martin, son of Henry and resident at Stoneleigh in 1901, was knighted in 1917. Banney Royd's Armitage was 'upwardly mobile' from Storalee in Murray Rd; when he retired to Bournemouth in 1919, the house was bought by Lt Col Emmanuel Hoyle, son of the manufacturer Joseph Hoyle of Longwood, who was made a baronet in 1922. His neighbour at Norwood, Joseph Henry Kaye, received the same honour in the following year (also the year of his death).[97]

Edgerton in 1911

ALONGSIDE THESE GRAND houses, however, the villa suburb was still very much in business as the Victorian era gave way to the Edwardian, and the 1911 Census allows a final glance at what Edgerton had become.

There had been very little fresh development since the 1880s. Four new semis at Sunny Side were tucked into the Lockwood land between 1893 and 1907, and Deveron House (see p.133) was added to Queen's Rd in 1906. Imperial Rd and Cleveland Rd, leading up from the main road towards Marsh, had been largely developed with terraced or semi-detached housing. Otherwise the high Victorian villas stood supreme, detached or semi-detached but almost entirely in single-family occupation, with a handful of schools as the only exceptions. The Census, for the first time, asked owners to identify the number of rooms, and the results (fig.36) are an interesting summary. Of 68 houses identifiable in this way (a few were empty, with nil returns), over half the houses had 12 or more rooms (including kitchens, but not sculleries, bathrooms or closets), with the 12-room house the most common size: villas but not mansions.

Occupations in 1911 were more diverse than among the first residents 50–60 years earlier. The textile trades remained dominant, if anything more so than in the 1860s, with numerous wool merchants, woollen and – by this time – worsted manufacturers and yarn spinners. The heads of major engineering businesses, Horace Broadbent and Frank Addy Hopkinson, were at Edgerton Grove and Willow Bank respectively. Others with 'trade' backgrounds included a brush manufacturer, a jeweller and a decorator's merchant, a coachmaker (William Rippon), two building contractors and a civil engineer. The financial sector continued to grow, with several bankers, a stockbroker and an accountant represented. The 'public service' professions were as yet little in evidence, though a school principal was a rare instance of a female head of household, and a 'director of multiple grocery stores' gives a glimpse of the inter-war years ahead. Service establishments could still be extensive: at Oakwood Charles Freeman, his wife and daughter were

Col. C. E. Freeman, J.P.

Fig.35
Charles Freeman of Oakwood, Hungerford Rd.

supported by a nurse, housemaid, parlour maid, laundry maid, kitchen maid and cook, though three servants was more typical.

NO OF ROOMS	NO OF HOUSES	NOTES
20	1	Edgerton Hill
19	1	Hazelgrove
18	1	Bankfield [and Clyde?]
17	3	Norwood, Buckden Mount, Ravensdeane
16	1	Banney Royd
15	5	
14	3	
13	8	
12	14	
11	6	
10	6	
9	10	
8	6	
7	3	

Fig.36
Rooms in Edgerton villas in the 1911 Census, with the largest identified.

In the wider world, these were troubled times. As Thomas Armstrong evoked it:

The uneasy pre-war world. Trade shocking, Von Tirpitz building a ridiculously large fleet, Bradford filled with Japs picking Yorkshire brains, Home Rule for Ireland splitting the land into two camps, suffragette outrages .... strike after strike by men who wanted nothing more than the food on which to live.[98]

Fig.37
Robert and Martha Fell and family at Somerville, probably on their golden wedding anniversary in 1904.
Three family members were in Canada at the time and were manually 'photoshopped' in: for further
information see www.faulder.org.uk/genealogy/?p=199

For some historians, Britain was as close to a social revolution as it had been since the 1840s, before the period of calm within which Edgerton had grown up. There was sufficient establishment anxiety, in July 1912, for King George V and Queen Mary – advised to do so by the Cabinet and the Archbishop of York – to undertake a Royal Tour of the North, in order to calm the natives. First port of call, in their half day in and around Huddersfield, was Horace Martin's Wellington Mills at Oakes, the town's largest employer – cementing the status of the Martins of Stoneleigh as the leading local family by then. Elsewhere in Edgerton, the suffragette Bertha Lowenthal lived at The Grange during the movement's bitter struggle with the Asquith government – directly opposite Ashleigh House, former home of Asquith's uncle James Willans. But there is little sense that Edgerton – or its fictional representation as Armstrong's 'Moorheaton' – was much touched by these great events. And of course the advent of war would soon change everything.

Beyond that lay the inter-war era, with renewed prosperity for the business class, when Huddersfield is often said to have had the highest density of Rolls-Royce ownership in the country. Certainly J H Kaye at Norwood had the second car registered in Lindley, a Panhard, in 1908, while Sir Emmanuel Hoyle's early 1920s Rolls, with coachwork by Rippons of Huddersfield, survives today in Liechtenstein![99] William Rippon the coachbuilder lived at Cedar Grove, Binham Rd. In the early 1950s, in similar vein, Norwood Grange hosted Lord Hanson's glamorous parties with stars of stage and screen during his brief engagement to Audrey Hepburn, while celebrated rally driver Anne Hall lived at Oak Hill (p.76).

But by then the era of opulence was over for most, giving way to post-war austerity and egalitarianism (itself now a thing of the past). Stoneleigh was a local authority care home; Banney Royd was a fire service college; Norwood would soon be demolished; and many other Edgerton houses were passing into new uses as student hostels or nursing homes. It would take another book to deal properly with these chapters in Edgerton's story.

Fig.38 (overleaf)
Edgerton gate piers.

Perambulation

THIS SECTION OFFERS *a house-by-house walking tour of the whole area. There is no perfect way to organise it. The approach taken here is to move outwards along Edgerton/Halifax Rd, from the Blacker Rd crossroads to Thornhill Rd and Bryan Rd, returning at the end to the Queen's Rd area. This offers a sequence which is logical and broadly chronological, but at the expense of several crossings of the main road; a full circuit is about two miles and to attend to every house could take a half day. The map [fig.50, pp.84/85] , with a key number for each house, should make other choices possible – or the tour could just be an 'armchair' one! The route uses only public rights of way and the privacy of occupiers must of course be respected.*

Edgerton Grove Road

STARTING AT THE traffic lights at Edgerton Rd/Blacker Rd, and turning south-west along Edgerton Grove Rd, three large houses are set back to the left on higher ground. These are the only houses built on Ramsden land which plausibly qualify as 'Edgerton villas' (albeit included in the Greenhead Park Conservation Area). Moving away from the junction, in turn these are Oak Hill, West Mount and Marsh Field. When they were built, in the late 1860s, they would have looked out across Blacker Lane (as it then was) onto Georgian Edgerton, including the drive of Edgerton Grove (fig.6, p.16). Today the view is of the Edgerton Green estate, built in the 1970s, with only the stone boundary wall to suggest the early C19 properties.

Fig.39
Mayfield and Grannum Lodge, Edgerton Rd, depicted in 1882 sale particulars.

Fig.40
West Mount, Edgerton Grove Rd.

Oak Hill (map ref. 1) is an attractive Gothic house which, from resemblance to work elsewhere, could easily be by John Kirk. **West Mount** and **Marsh Field (2)**, a pair of large semis, were designed by W H Crossland, who deployed an interesting range of medieval motifs on what is essentially a more stolid building than Oak Hill.[100] All three were originally owned by a solicitor, Henry Barker: he was a member of the building committee of St Andrew's Church, Leeds Rd, for which Crossland was also the architect.[101] Barker was at Marsh Field in 1871 – when he was elected a 'Church' member of the School Board – and at West Mount in 1874. By 1888 his business was evidently in deep trouble and, declared bankrupt, he fled his creditors.[102]

At that point his tenant at Oak Hill was professor of music Henry Parratt, a celebrated family name in Huddersfield musical circles. He was the son

Fig.41
Oak Hill, Edgerton Grove Rd.

NORTH ELEVATION

Fig.42
Elevation of West Mount,
by W H Crossland.

of Thomas, the Parish Church organist, and older brother of Walter, who was knighted in 1892 and became Master of the Queen's Music in 1893. Henry Parratt was himself "an extremely talented musician and it was only his uncertain health that prevented him equalling, in some measure, the achievements of his eminent brother".[103] His sister Emily ran a school at Oak Hill from 1877, moving to nearby Grannum Lodge by 1911. By then worsted manufacturer Alfred Sykes was at Oak Hill and James Wallace, director of multiple grocery shops – 'the people's grocers, branches everywhere' – at Marsh Field. Another grocer, Richard Smith Dyson, acquired West Mount and Marsh Field from Barker's mortgagees in 1899 and lived at West Mount until his death in 1909.

Edgerton Road

RETURNING TO AND crossing the main road – named simply 'Edgerton' until the 1960s – and turning left, five houses on the right-hand side were built on land once owned by Thomas Varley of Edgerton House, the blocked-up entrance to which can be seen across the road on the left.

First are **Mayfield** & **Grannum Lodge (3)** (listed, grade II; also gate piers), a pair of magnificent Gothic houses, now further divided, which it seems misleading to call 'semi-detached'. That is what they are, but with Mayfield facing the main road and Grannum facing Blacker Rd, each can easily be read as a large detached villa. Particularly striking features are the stepped gables, the pillared and gabled portals to both houses, and the three-storey tower of Grannum – though the steeply pitched roof of the tower, visible in 1882 (fig.39) has been replaced by a less imposing flat one. Although sometimes attributed to John Kirk in 1883, in fact they were certainly standing by 1864, and may be by Pritchett & Sons; the firm had previously drawn up proposals for a larger number of villas on the site (see p.28), and purchasers were directed to their offices.[104] (On the other hand, the Gothic cottage at 202 Blacker Rd (listed II) is by Kirk, for the same client.) While Mayfield is close to the main road, Grannum is set well back from Blacker Rd beyond what early maps (figs.3,14) show as Blacker (or Blacker Lane) Wood, with a stream running through it. Its unusual name – an archaic term for grandmother – recalls Grannam Croft, which appears in the 1801 land sale (p.14).

Sale particulars in 1882 when the freehold was marketed with sitting tenants, describe how each house contains:

Spacious entrance hall, vestibule, side hall, drawing room, dining room, breakfast room, 8 bedrooms and dressing rooms. Bathrooms, butler's pantry, lavatory, domestic offices, store rooms and cellars in the basement. .... Greenhouse, potting shed, stable, harness room and coachhouse. .... The grounds are well arranged with tennis lawn, ornamental pleasure grounds, shrubberies, and are easily accessible from the town and railway station.[105]

Fig.43
Grannum House & Lodge
(top) and Mayfield (bottom),
Edgerton Rd.

Fig.44
A gate pier of demolished
Edgerton House outside
Bankfield.

Fig.45
Clyde House (foreground) &
Bankfield, Edgerton Rd.

The client for this magnificence was William Clarke, a John William St surgeon, who let the houses out. As tenanted properties they had quite a high turnover of residents. Grannum's C19 tenants included a series of woollen manufacturers – Thomas Learoyd, Joseph Wrigley and Joah Lodge – while successively at Mayfield were Ramsden agent Capt Thomas Brook, wool merchants Robert Skilbeck and Thomas Aked, and other medical men. Skilbeck was the last chairman of Huddersfield Improvement Commissioners, in 1867/8, before that body was replaced by Huddersfield Corporation; he moved out to Crosland Hall, Netherton early in the 1870s. Although Dr Clarke died in 1875, the freehold remained with his family until 1910.

Next come **Clyde House** & **Bankfield (4)** (listed II; also gate piers), two austere and honestly semi-detached houses with extensive classical detailing, unusually including a balustrade along the roof-line, and still with the blackened stonework largely eliminated elsewhere. These were built by a Bradford fancy manufacturer, Abraham Hopkinson, as an investment and rented out. Distinctive in style, they were perhaps designed by Edward Wyndham Tarn, who sought tenders to build two houses in Edgerton in February 1862. They were under construction in December 1862, when building worker William Byram fell from the scaffold, by no means a unique occurrence.[106]

The first tenant of Clyde House, until the 1880s, was Maximilian Zossenheim, a Jewish shipping agent from northern Germany (whose middle name was Clyde). After that, Frank Walker, a sealskin and mantle cloth manufacturer, was briefly a resident, as was woollen manufacturer Henry Middlemost. Meanwhile Bankfield was the first married home of Joseph (later Sir Joseph) Crosland. He was a member of the large woollen manufacturing firm of his father George Crosland (of Crosland Lodge, Blackmoorfoot Rd), for whom Britannia Buildings in St George's Square was built as a warehouse. But his stay in Edgerton was brief: he soon built and moved to Royds Wood, Paddock (now the nucleus of Royds Hall School), had an extensive career in local public life and was briefly Conservative MP for Huddersfield in 1893–5, following in the footsteps of his brother T P Crosland of Gledholt. By 1871 the German merchants James and Joseph Liebreich were the tenants of Bankfield, moving there from Edgerton Lodge. They were followed by a family of Hirsts; James Hirst, cotton spinner, was resident until the 1930s. As well as its own gate piers, Bankfield boasts a supernumary one, displaying the fading legend 'Edgerton House' (fig.44), on whose former land it stands, presumably moved there from the other side of the road after the latter was demolished.

The next house, **Edgerton Bank (5)**, is unlisted but more playful than its neighbours, sporting an asymmetric front with a Dutch gable above a doorway with a distinctively blocky 'Gibbs surround'. It is one of the first Victorian houses, built around 1851 as an investment by Benjamin Casson, who was high bailiff at the county court (newly established in 1847 at the Court House in Queen St), and retained by his executors. A long succession of tenants of the fairly modest house included the solicitor John Freeman

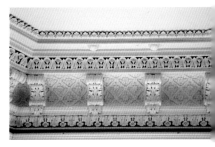

Fig.46
Bankfield, Edgerton Rd: hall, dining room and drawing room.

Fig.47
Edgerton Bank, Edgerton Rd.

Fig.48
Bremen House, Edgerton Rd.

(later of Oakwood, Hungerford Rd); Julius Zossenheim, a shipping agent like his brother Max at Clyde House; Robert Learoyd, of the Leeds Rd manufacturers; Alfred Kaye of Kayes Drapers, which survived until 1982, and chemical manufacturer Sidney Abbey.

Moving from Varley to Fenton land, next comes **Bremen House (6)** (listed II; also gate piers), a substantial Italianate house of 1868 with a characteristic observation tower. It was built for King St wine merchant Richard Rhodes, moving uphill from Newhouse, and the unusual name presumably reflects the port from which he imported German wines. Certainly Rhodes' trade is reflected in the carving of grapes in the gate piers and doorcase, which also has fine granite shafts, and before conversion to flats the motif reportedly continued in "magnificent frescoes" on the ceilings.[107] The architect was perhaps William Cocking,[108] who certainly designed the stables and coach house (now no.14a). Unfortunately Rhodes died within weeks of taking up residence; the house was advertised for sale 'as new', and the sale particulars (fig.49) give a nice glimpse into the quality of a newly-erected Edgerton villa as depicted by the agent.

The house was taken by Ellen Sykes, widow of Edward Grocock Sykes, one of the brothers of the well-known Lindley industrial dynasty, and their son William, who moved the short distance 'up' from Ebor Mount, New North Rd (a fine terrace of four houses by Kirk). Edward had managed Russian cotton mills and William was born in Moscow in 1848. He became a cotton spinner in a Sykes business at Albany Mills and later a wool broker, living at several other local houses including Burbank (Thornhill Rd) and Glenwood (Halifax Rd).[109] The Sykes were followed at Bremen House by a corn miller, John Hirst and then by Edward Mallinson, G W Shaw and, by 1911, James Willans JP, formerly of Ashleigh (see p.107) and lately of Rose Hill. The house was renamed West Lodge for a while, perhaps by Mallinson.

Across Queen's Rd are a pair of Gothic semis, **Elm Crest** & **Burleigh** (7) (listed II) – again set at right-angles to enhance their status – but 'deceptively spacious' anyway, as the estate agents say, with Elm Crest boasting ten bedrooms in 2010.[110] These were built around 1865 by John William Walker, a New St linen draper, in a modestly Gothic style with distinctive 'Caernarvon-arched' (shouldered) windows. Elm Crest (originally Elm Lea), facing Queen's Rd, was occupied by John Walker, while his younger brother Frederick, a wool salesman, took Burleigh. By 1881 the leaseholder was James Eastwood, wool merchant, who lived at Burleigh, while solicitor George Lewis Batley came to live at Elm Lea. Eastwood's widow was still at Burleigh in 1911, by which time woollen manufacturer Frederick Ellis was at Elm Lea. In recent *Examiner* property coverage both have become 'mill-owners' houses', the default assumption for every Edgerton home.

Whilst continuing along Edgerton Rd, a glance across to the opposite side provides a clear view of the drive of **Edgerton Hill** (8) (listed II), the

Sales by Auction.

BREMEN HOUSE, EDGERTON, NEAR HUDDERSFIELD.
TO BE SOLD BY AUCTION, BY Mr. THORNTON, at the George Hotel, Huddersfield, on Tuesday evening, 29th September, at Six for Seven prompt,

ALL that excellent newly-erected stone-built MANSION, situate at Edgerton, Huddersfield, called Bremen House, containing on the basement floor large and well lighted kitchen, laundry, fitted with Ormsen's patent jointless tubular boiler and steam piping for drying cloths; extensive keeping, wine, coal, and other cellars; on the ground floor, entrance porch, vestibule, corridor, paved with encaustic tiles of an elegant pattern, spacious dining-room, ante-room, and conservatory, beautiful drawing-room, also breakfast and smoking-rooms, w. c., cloakroom, butler's pantry and storeroom.

A most handsome staircase, lighted with a large window, upon which are painted four beautiful landscapes, leads up to the first floor, which contains six good-sized and lofty bedrooms and two dressing-rooms, one of which is fitted up with bath, &c.; housemaid's closet and water-closet on the second floor, six good bedrooms and a storeroom, two large wrought-iron water cisterns, capable of holding upwards of 500 gallons each.

The whole of the entertaining rooms and the bedrooms on the first floor are excellently fitted up with marble mantle-pieces and fire grates of superior quality, and the whole of the ceilings are richly decorated. There is also a hot water apparatus, for heating the house.

The house is built upon an eminence, beautifully situated, and commands extensive views down the valley of the Colne, and of the surrounding neighbourhood. A nice garden encircles the house.

The internal arrangements are excellent, all the fittings and appointments being of the best description, and good taste has been displayed in the decorations.

The house is fitted up with gas, and is supplied with water from the Huddersfield Water Works. The drainage is amply provided for, and conveyed into a sewer in Queen's-road, upon which road the estate adjoins on the north side.

The Estate comprises an area of 5,176 square yards, and is fenced in with a substantial lime-built stone wall, massive iron entrance gates, and stone posts.

The Land, except a small quantity at the entrance (which is freehold), is held under lease from the trustees of Lewis Fenton, Esq., deceased, for 999 years.

Plans and particulars are in course of preparation, and will be ready on the 14th September. Further particulars and tickets to view may be obtained on application to the Auctioneer, or to Messrs. Brook and Nephew, surveyors, Huddersfield; or to

Messrs. LAYCOCK, DYSON, and LAYCOCK,
Solicitors, Huddersfield.

Fig.49
Sale particulars for Bremen House, 1868.

one survivor of 'Georgian Edgerton'; unfortunately the house is not easily viewed from the road (private drives should of course not be entered without permission). As mentioned above (p.19), this house was erected around 1820, in a plain Georgian style with a well-proportioned round bay, by linen draper Frederick Hudson. He died in 1824 and was succeeded by general merchant John Haigh and (Methodist) brewer Thomas Wilson before the house became the Edgerton 'seat' of the Armitage family (see p.46) by 1839.[111] Remaining until Alfred, the last Armitage to live there, died in 1923, they substantially enlarged the house to accommodate a big family. There is a Victorian extension of no architectural pretension, perhaps linking the house to an earlier stables block, and in the early 1880s Edward Hughes designed an imposing Classical porch and a billiard room, awkwardly joined to the main body of the house. The 1871 Census records seven indoor servants and three outdoor, who occupied the three terraced cottages set in the grounds at an angle to the main road a little way beyond the entrance. After the departure of the Armitages another famous Colne Valley mill-owning family came to Edgerton Hill, with William Alfred Crowther (formerly of The Mount – see p.88) there in the mid-1920s, and it was from the Crowthers that the Ukrainian Club bought the property in the 1960s.

Falling away from the road to the right here is the much-contested open space of **Clayton Fields**. It was owned until 1852 by Thomas Robinson, heir to the Holroyds of Birkby Grange,[112] thereafter by his trustees and in the C20 by Tom Herbert Kaye of nearby Glenside (see p.95) who reputedly attempted to levy a charge for tobogganing there. Some years before his death in 1937 Kaye released a plot for development and a pair of stone semis, Brook House was built, designed by Leonard Burland OBE.[113] Kaye's executors sold the remaining land in 1957 to a builder and developer, George Haigh; his 1960s planning permissions are only now being activated, after an epic legal struggle by the Clayton Fields Action Group to maintain the space for its customary informal leisure uses. Why the Fields remained largely undeveloped for so long, bordering the Lockwood and Fenton lands, is unclear – perhaps the site was judged too wet to build on. It is interesting

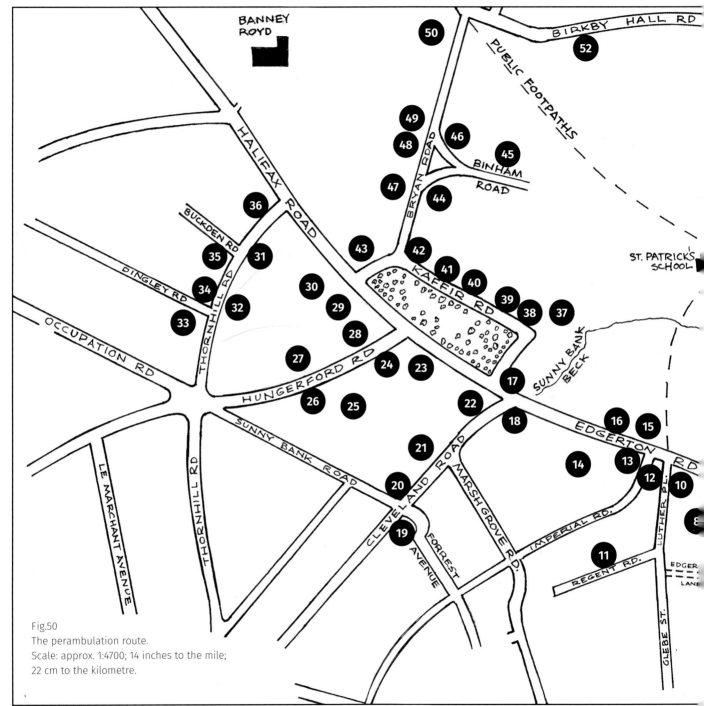

Fig.50
The perambulation route.
Scale: approx. 1:4700; 14 inches to the mile;
22 cm to the kilometre.

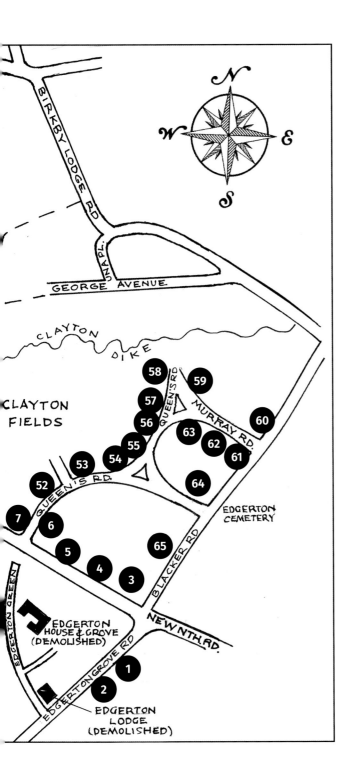

The Villas of Edgerton

1	Oak Hill	33	Burbank & Fernleigh
2	Marsh Field & West Mount	34	Buckden Mount
		35	Thorn Hill
3	Grannum Lodge/ House & Mayfield	36	Springfield
		37	Lunnclough Hall
4	Bankfield & Clyde House	38	Hollinhurst & Holmwood
5	Edgerton Bank	39	Woodlands
6	Bremen House	40	Brantwood & Oakleigh
7	Burleigh House & Elm Crest	41	Bryan Croft
		42	Low Wood
8	Edgerton Hill	43	The Grange
9	Tram shelter	44	Bryan Wood
10	Edgerton Cottage	45	Cedar Grove
11	Oak Lea	46	Binham Lodge & Thornleigh
12	Roseneath & Rose Bank	47	Bryan Lodge & Woodleigh
13	The Mount		
14	The Knowle & Woodville	48	Oakfield Lodge
15	Waverley	49	Beechwood
16	Edgerton Villa	50	Stoneleigh
17	Glenwood	51	Rose Hill
18	Glenside	52	Bankfield & Springfield
19	Glen View	53	Deveron House
20	Sunny Bank	54	Burnieside
21	Cleveland House	55	Sedgefield
22	Willow Bank	56	Holly Bank & Westoe
23	Hungerford House	57	Elmford
24	Oakley House	58	Laurence Dene & Storalee
25	Laurel Bank		
26	Granville	59	Fernbrook
27	Somerville	60	Elm Grove
28	Oakwood	61	Woodside
29	Cote Royd	62	Glen Villa
30	Ashleigh & Trafford House	63	Strathmore
		64	Wood Field
31	Ravensdeane	65	Ellerslie
32	The Gables		

to note, however, that the Fields are now being developed not by a single builder but through the sale – albeit freehold rather than leasehold – of individual plots, in a return to the 19th century development model.

Next is the Huddersfield Corporation tram shelter (9) (listed II) a striking late Victorian feature.[114] Adjacent is one of the milestones erected by the Improvement Commissioners to enable the calculation of hackney cab fares. Once viewed, the route of the perambulation crosses Edgerton Rd via the nearby pedestrian crossing.

On the corner of Luther Place, adjacent to the servants' cottages of Edgerton Hill, is **Edgerton Cottage (10)**. Despite its name, this is larger than it looks from the front, having been completed in two phases in 1848 and 1852 – the first of the Lockwood leases. It is in a plain, four-square style which could as easily be late Georgian as early Victorian. The first leaseholder was a Westgate innkeeper, Robert Spivey, landlord of the Green Dragon in Westgate, who may briefly have lived there himself; but from 1852 the enlarged house was home to George Henry Brook and his son George Smith Brook. The former, who died in 1882, was an insurance agent after the demise of the wool brokerage in which he was a partner (which caused him to 'downsize' from Edgerton Lodge), while the latter was actuary to the Huddersfield and Upper Agbrigg Savings Bank for 42 years, until his death in 1925.

A short detour along Luther Place and its continuation, Glebe St, is worthwhile for several reasons. First, there is a glimpse on the left of Edgerton Hill. Second, the public footpath bounding that property (pictured on p.17) is Edgerton Lane, running to the site (at the bend) of Edgerton House/Grove and, before them, of the ancient Edgerton settlement. Beyond the footpath the modern social housing development of Spire Court occupies what was the playing field of Waverley School (see p.90) and, before that, the glebe land of Huddersfield Parish Church – hence the street name.[115] This was originally 8.5 acres, including the site of the turn-of-the-century terraced housing opposite, which was developed by the Armitage family. Finally, on the opposite side of Luther Place in Regent Rd – originally Leonard Place – are some more substantial houses, including the double-fronted Italianate

Fig.51
Tram shelter, Edgerton Rd.

Oak Lea (11) (9 Regent Rd, listed II; also gate piers). This was designed in 1869 by John Kirk for Henry Haigh, woollen merchant, who was still there in 1911. Kirk's decoratively incised lintel here is a motif repeated at Bankfield, Queen's Rd (see p.132).

Returning to the main road, next are the unmatched semis **Roseneath** (originally **Ashfield House**) & **Rose Bank (12)** (listed II), with Roseneath fronting to Luther Place. With its Gothic bay and crenellated parapet, this building makes the most of its cramped site between Luther Place and Imperial Rd. The 1849 Lockwood lease was to Patrick Martin (see p.45), who was in occupation by 1851, as were three sisters named Berry at Rose Bank – then Rose Cottage. Martin moved away around 1859 but retained the lease and returned for another spell, with his housekeeper Mary Dawson occupying Rose Bank in 1871. By the late 1880s Ashfield was home to

Fig.52
Roseneath and (behind)
Rose Bank, Halifax Rd.

timber merchant Herbert Smith Brook, whose brother George was next door at Edgerton Cottage, and whose widow Ada remained until moving two doors the other way, to 2 The Mount, by 1900. After their departure it was renamed Roseneath.

From this point we reach the "six houses building" noted in the 1851 Census. Continuing on the left side of the main road, up a short drive from Imperial Rd and set back behind trees, are two large Greek Revival semis, 1 & 2 **The Mount (13)** (listed II – formerly Mount Edgerton), with imposing Ionic-pillared porticos. They were built around 1851 by boot and shoe makers Henry and John Liddell, and Henry lived at No 1 himself until his death in 1866; thereafter they were rented out by their trustees, until the lease was bought by Janet Martin, daughter-in-law of Patrick. At No 1 German merchant Henry Anders was followed by manufacturer Alfred Blackburn, a shareholder in the Martins' business at Wellington Mills – it sported a 50-foot aviary in his time – and by 1900 Henry Bull MA was running a boys' school there. At No 2 the successive tenants were a woollen manufacturer named Schofield; banker Edwin Last; and by 1900 Ada Brook, moving from Edgerton Cottage. She was followed by Alfred (W A) Crowther before his

Fig.53
Woodville (left) and The Knowle, Halifax Rd.

move to Edgerton Hill. In the moves and inter-relationships of Brooks, Martins and Crowthers among five successive houses along Edgerton Rd, one catches a glimpse of the densely inter-twined world of these neighbouring families.

Another pair of semis built on Lockwood land follows, with a lease from 1849 and built around 1851; originally these were both named **Woodville** (listed II), a common practice, but the second is now **The Knowle (14)**. Hidden from the road up curving drives (fig.18), these are ashlar houses in a restrained Tudor style, built back-to-back, with parapeted bays, a fishscale roof and bargeboarded gables; The Knowle has been substantially extended. According to John Brook, the first was built by land agent Frederick Holroyd and the second by architect James Radcliffe. However, as both these gentlemen were engaged by the Thornhill estate, one wonders if perhaps Holroyd was the developer and Radcliffe (chiefly a mill architect) the designer of the houses. The first was initially let to wool merchant Foster Shaw and then to John Brooke Greenwood, a shipping merchant also described as an amateur poet and writer. In 1863 it was bought by Joshua Whitworth, a tea merchant based in the Packhorse Yard and in Mincing Lane, London and a member of Marsh Local Board in its final year. An entertaining report in the *Chronicle* of a dinner held there for his staff in 1868 (fig.54), suggests he was something of a character. In 1873 he secured a surprise victory in the Liberal interest in a Council by-election; by 1891 iron and steel merchant Henry Taylor had replaced him at Woodville.

The Knowle, once called Holly Mount, was first used as a clergy house for St Paul's Church, with Revd John Haigh resident in 1861, but was soon owned by Henry Fischer, another German wool merchant and one more following the uphill path from Belgrave Terrace; his partner Edward Huth lived at Oakfield Lodge (see p.125). Fischer died in 1880, to be followed by rag paper merchant James Waddington and machine-maker William Whiteley. By 1908 William Henry Heywood, glazing engineer, and family were at Holly Mount, and made a handsome donation to the Infirmary.

Fig.54
A jolly dinner at Woodville, 1868.

Fig.55
Waverley (front), Edgerton Rd.

The Heywood Williams firm survived into the 21st century, eventually occupying nearby **Waverley (15)**, reached by crossing the road and resuming from the tram shelter. It was built as Hazelgrove (listed II; also gate piers) on a two-and-a-half acre plot with a long boundary wall to Clayton Fields. Since 1936 it has been home to Waverley School (whence today's name), then to Heywood Williams, and now to 13 apartments. After successive modifications it could almost be taken for a C20 neo-Georgian building, which in part it is (see below). In fact it was built as two houses at the start

Fig.56
Waverley (rear), Edgerton Rd.

of the 1850s, the right-hand one becoming Hazeldene by 1889. The original plan comprised two long, narrow houses, each two rooms deep and three bays long. They were entered from a central covered single-storey section, apparently approached by a raised drive from the old carriage road beyond Clayton Dike (see p.122) as well as from the main road.[116] This enabled each house to have front and rear elevations of three segmental bays, uninterrupted by doorways – twelve bays in all. Unusual classical, almost Egyptian detail was employed throughout, with a motif of roundels between the windows and pylon-shaped window surrounds. The design is unlike anything else locally and the absence of an architect's name is regrettable.

The rippling rhythm of six bays at the rear (fig.56) can still be glimpsed from Sunny Side (see p.93), but the front elevation has been substantially changed, in a complex building history. In 1877 both houses were thrust forward by symmetrical entrance wings, designed by John Kirk; in 1893 the redundant central entrance was replaced by a billiard room, again by Kirk, with the extra space included in the left-hand house; and in 1912 Willie

Cooper disrupted the symmetry of the front by tucking in a new drawing room to the left of the entrance wing (later matched on the right). The school, first occupying Hazelgrove and then the whole building, made further changes, including a disfiguring fire escape, but closed in 1987. Heywood Williams then made it a showcase for their aluminium windows; their use caused some concern to conservation officers, but on the other hand the company carefully applied the distinctive features of the original design to the entire facade for the first time (though the added central portico is ill-judged).

The leasehold owners throughout the C19 were the Upperhead Row manufacturer Joshua Lockwood and his business partners and successors in the Keighley family. Lockwood lived in one house himself until his death in 1862, and Charles Keighley JP, Lockwood's grandson, was there in the 1880s. Their business was the large woollen factory at Upperhead Row, specialising in corduroy and other heavy fabrics and eventually covering three acres; Lockwood lived on site at Upperhead House before moving to Hazelgrove. A Whig and a Wesleyan, Lockwood was a member of several of the town's early public bodies, though not a particularly active one (the larger manufacturers rarely were – building their businesses was no doubt enough to keep them occupied). Two generations on, Charles Keighley was a Tory and eventually an Anglican, again with a modest career in public office.

Other C19 tenants of one or other house included woollen manufacturers James Crosland, who served on the reinvigorated Marsh Local Board from 1866–8, and went on to build Royds Mount in Luck Lane, now Huddersfield Grammar School; Ephraim Taylor, later at Cedar Grove; Alfred & Godfrey Crowther, who moved 'up' to Rose Hill; and Hyram Dyson. By 1891 Keighley had moved to Greenhead (Dalton), a mansion in 14 acres of land, and solicitor Archibald Fletcher was at Hazelgrove, which offered five "entertaining rooms" and 10 bedrooms,[117]

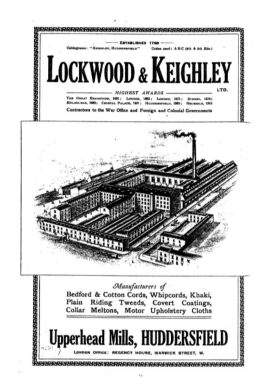

Fig.57
Mill advert by the owners of Waverley (then Hazelgrove), circa 1915.

while retired cotton broker Robert Cameron (moving *from* Rose Hill) was at Hazeldene. Fletcher was followed by manufacturers Joseph (later Sir Joseph) Henry Kaye (see p.66), before his move to Norwood around 1900, and Sydney Brierley, while Cameron's successor was mill manager Arthur Jabez Brook. In summary, these were handsome and distinctive houses, available to let and well suited to professional men and their families or as stepping stones in a businessman's ascent towards a grander mansion a little further out.

Next is **Edgerton Villa** (**16**) (listed II; also gate piers), a much plainer neo-classical house which was briefly added to Waverley School before its closure in the 1980s, and is now let out as offices. Built on a Lockwood lease of 1850, and not a grand house, this is recorded in the 1851 Census as housing King St linen draper Robert Owen, his mother, wife, five children and no fewer than seven assistant or apprentice drapers. Also present were woolstapler Thomas Hirst, his wife and servant, soon to move to Willow Bank (see p.98). By 1855 the house was divided between Owen and schoolmaster James Hanson, Huddersfield College boarders replacing the apprentices. A longer-term resident from around 1860 until the 1880s was wool merchant Charles Johnson, later a manufacturer at Wooldale, followed by 1891 by insurance manager Joseph Mills. The owner in 1911, decorator's merchant Albert Greenwood, was father to future Yorkshire cricket and hockey captain Frank Greenwood, then aged 5.

After two semis of around 1900 (26 & 28 Edgerton Rd), a brief detour down Sunny Side is worthwhile (especially in the winter months with less tree cover). To the right is the rear view of Waverley mentioned above, while a glance to the left, across the Sunny Bank Beck, affords the best available view of Lunnclough Hall in Kaffir Rd (see p.115). Continuing on the main road, the Beck's deep ravine can also be seen just before the next house is reached, emphasising the height of the embankment needed to carry the turnpike road across it. The Beck was the boundary between the parishes and townships of Huddersfield and Lindley, and in the 1860s between the territories of the short-lived Local Boards for Marsh and Lindley (see pp.60–61).

Beyond the ravine **Glenwood (17)** (listed II; also gate piers), though strictly speaking the first house (No 2) in Halifax Rd, is also the last before the substantial gap formed by Edgerton Park (p.114), and so is best treated here. Having crossed into Lindley, once part of the manor of Fixby, it is also the first house on Thornhill land. Like Waverley its building history is complex. Built by 1856, it was originally a handsome but straightforwardly rectangular ashlar-faced villa, enhanced by a steep 'park' descending to the beck – a horse belonging to Read Holliday of Lunnclough Hall (p.115) fell 40 or 50 feet to its death there in 1872, emphasising the drama of the terrain.[118] The two-storey canted bay on the front was added in 1880 by Edward Hughes, who also designed the stables and coach house round the corner in Kaffir Rd; perhaps the curious blind windows on the entrance facade date from this time too. Then came a three-storey addition

Fig.58
Glenwood, Halifax Rd.

at the rear left, making good use of the sloping site (by Ben Stocks, 1883), which was extended forward to align with the front elevation in 1912 by J W Cocking and Frank Abbey; this portion is now the separate Colt House (2A Halifax Rd).

The first lessee was wool merchant Joseph Shaw, who served as Huddersfield township's chief constable in 1856–8. On his election to what was, by then, a largely ceremonial post, overshadowed by the chairman of the Improvement Commissioners, Shaw summoned a dozen or more of his neighbouring worthy gentlemen to a banquet at Glenwood, "to uphold the dignity and support the prestige of the office ... The display on the table was ample and choice, embracing every delicacy procurable for the season, and the hospitality and courteous bearing of the entertainer elicited the admiration of all present."[119] Shaw was succeeded at Glenwood in 1863 by the bookseller and stationer Joseph Brook, whose widow remained until 1893. Brook was the third generation in this line of business, with a shop in Westgate from the early C19 which also served as the Stamp Office, where official documents were endorsed. Like Shaw he was quite prominent in public life, as a churchwarden, Improvement Commissioner and Infirmary Governor.[120] By 1901 it was retirement home to William Sykes (see p.82), and his son Charles Frederick Sykes JP, 'plush, astrahkhan, sealskin and ladies' mantle manufacturer', died there in 1915, leaving £114,208.[121]

Turning the corner into Kaffir Rd affords perhaps the best available view of castellated Willow Bank opposite (see p.98).

Cleveland Road

BEFORE CONTINUING ON Halifax Rd, a short detour up Cleveland Rd is worthwhile. To its left, today's undistinguished mid-1970s housing association development occupies the site of **Glenside (18)**, one of the few houses that have been lost, though gate piers and adjacent outbuildings remain at the street corner. It may be the house referred to in the *Chronicle* in 1857 as one that, in contrast to its neighbours, "suffers considerably from poverty of detail".[122] Built around 1851 for Holmfirth manufacturer and merchant James Hinchliffe, it passed to Revd Joel Mallinson, a Wesleyan minister, in 1885; author of *The History of Methodism in Huddersfield, Holmfirth and Denby Dale* (1893), he remained until 1908. Subsequently it was home, until his death in 1937, to Tom Herbert Kaye, a self-made man, described in his obituary as "accountant, company director and cinema exhibitor", but also with substantial property interests including Clayton Fields and Willow Bank.

To the left, the tree cover around the housing association flats gives little sense now of the "charming glen" promised in 1881 sale particulars for Glenside.[123] At the corner of Forrest Avenue, however, is **Glen View (19)**, a gently Gothic house built around 1865 for Longwood stone merchant James Whitaker, originally as another disguised pair of right-angled semis, now combined as a residential home. When first built its north-east front would indeed have had an uninterrupted view down the glen, though an 'ornamental lodge' (now demolished) was built opposite for Thomas Hirst of Willow Bank around 1870, and Forrest Avenue itself driven across the glen in 1890, realigning and replacing an earlier footpath to Croft House.[124]

Fig.59
Joseph Hopkinson of Cleveland House.

Fig.60
Cleveland House, Cleveland Rd.

Fig.61
The 19th century arms of Berlin, depicted in stone at Cleveland House.

Beyond Glen View is the late C19 development of Cleveland Rd, running up into Marsh. On the diagonally opposite corner, however, the handsome Georgian **Sunny Bank (20)** (listed II) survives as two houses today (4 and 6 Cleveland Rd). In the first half of the C19 it was a larger building – indeed what remains may have grown from a row of linked cottages or a service wing, with the main house demolished early in the C20.[125] It was home to cloth dressers and farmers, typifying the rural dual economy: the 1854 OS map shows tenter fields, for cloth drying, between the house and the turnpike, where Cleveland House now stands, and in April 1864 cows, pigs, farming and dairy implements were auctioned there.[126]

By then, however, the freehold had been acquired by the Thornhill estate, enabling them to grant an 1863 lease for what is now **Cleveland House (21)** (listed II; also gate piers). The richly varied architectural detail here – Tuscan piers and entablatures, Doric porch, Anglo-Saxon or Medieval carved heads, French casement window – make this a prime example of mid-Victorian eclecticism. Originally it was Berlin House, built for German merchant Maximilian Liebmann, and the elaborate arms above the cornice are those of the city of Berlin in the 19th century. Next there, after 1870, was woollen manufacturer and churchwarden John Barnicot, who sold up to move to Shepley in 1885.[127] After brief occupancy by John William Martin of Wellington Mills (see p.45 for the Martins), by 1896 it was home to Joseph Hopkinson, founder of the celebrated Hopkinsons engineering firm and family; he died in 1907 but his widow, Ann and family remained until the 1920s.

Today Cleveland House is one of Edgerton's several nursing homes; when it came to market in 1987 it was described as "One of the few remaining Victorian residences still in use as a private house...almost completely restored and refurbished to its original magnificence", and by then comprising seven living rooms and eight bedrooms.[128] Returning to the main road, there is a glimpse of the billiard room and redbrick garden wall at the next house, Willow Bank, also occupied by a member of the Hopkinson family early in the C20.

Halifax Road & Hungerford Road

ON THE CORNER of Cleveland Rd and Halifax Rd, **Willow Bank (22)** (listed II), with its spectacular castellated Gothic tower and other crenellated features, is among the grandest of Edgerton houses and one of the few

Fig.62
Willow Bank, Halifax Rd.

to feature in George Sheeran's *Brass Castles*.[129] Sheeran briefly notes its "hall and cross-wing" plan form, while the list description praises "Much naturalistic carving (including rainwater heads) of high quality"; the fish-scale roof is also striking, but little of the detail is visible from the road. A billiard room was added on the Cleveland Rd side in 1896 by John Lunn of Milnsbridge, linking the house to the hothouse. Not only the house but the gate piers, boundary wall, crenellated archway and lodge are listed, grade II.

The leaseholder here from 1855 until his death in 1881 was wool merchant Thomas Hirst, whose monogram TCH adorns the entrance porch. His father Henry established the business in Chancery Lane and, as it grew, Thomas built the town centre's splendid Standard House as his warehouse.[130] His wife was Jane Sykes, sister of the industrialist Sykes brothers of Lindley, and indeed the first lease is to James Nield & Joseph Sykes, who may have had it built for the newly-weds (they had started their married life lodging at Edgerton Villa) but assigned it to Hirst in 1863.[131] Mrs Hirst died in July 1886 and sales soon followed of the sumptuous furnishings of the house, garden statuary and the extensive art collection: Hirst had been a significant collector and the auction of 110 works in October 1886 was described by the *Chronicle* as "one of the finest collections ever offered in the provinces" with "many well-known faces in the art world present".[132] The prices realised ranged from 20 up to 300 guineas, the latter for 'Temptation' by Briton Riviere RA.

Hirst's son Thomas Edward, a captain (later lieutenant-colonel) in the Duke of Wellington's Regiment, married Annette Scott weeks later, on 29 December 1886, and they retained the house until 1896. Having disposed of his parent's furnishings, the house was "expensively fitted and decorated" by the noted Arts & Crafts architect G Faulkner Armitage (see fig.63 overleaf),[133] whose work at Stoneleigh is discussed below (p.127). The buyer in 1896 was manufacturer John Edward Crowther, who commissioned the billiard room, but by 1898 Willow Bank was home to Frank Learoyd, fancy worsted manufacturer (of Trafalgar Mills, Leeds Rd) and from 1904 until his death in 1917 to Frank Hopkinson, chairman of the major engineering business, J Hopkinson & Co of Birkby.

Fig.63 (overleaf)
Eight Willow Bank photographs, perhaps c 1915, from a Hopkinson family album.
The interiors are those designed and supplied by Faulkner Armitage c1886.

Three contrasting houses then follow as one approaches and turns left into Hungerford Rd. First comes **Hungerford House (23)** (listed II; also gate piers), well-concealed up a drive off the main road. The first lease here dated from 1855 and the first tenant was George Pitt, another wool merchant (in partnership with Foster Shaw of Woodville); he was followed by a relative of Thomas Hirst next door and, by 1900, by cotton spinner Thomas Hudson. On the same leasehold plot, but accessed from Hungerford Rd and now occupied by Ramsdens the solicitors, is **Oakley House (24)** (listed II; also gate piers), first occupied around 1860 by the brick and tile manufacturer Edward Brooke JP. Variously known as 'the boss of Fieldhouse' – where his works was, off Leeds Rd – and 'Squire Brooke', reflecting his family roots in the land-owning Brookes of Honley, he founded the business and left it to his son in order to concentrate on his other life as a Wesleyan preacher. The son, also Edward, a prominent local Liberal, was still there in 1900, followed by bank manager Alfred Roberts. Next again on the left is **Laurel Bank (25)** (listed II; also gate piers and lamp post), renamed Bryancliffe for

Fig.64
Hungerford House, Halifax Rd.

a while but now back to its original name. This was first owned by Joseph Brooke Turner, a Lockwood wool merchant and manufacturer,[134] and from 1881 by John H Sykes, a woollen manufacturer at Gosport Mills, Outlane.

These three houses – not the grandest in Edgerton – offer in miniature the mid-Victorian 'battle of the styles'. Hungerford is a neo-classical ashlar-faced house with canted bays, a Tuscan-columned porch and hipped roof, similar to Ashleigh and Trafford House further along the main road (see p.107). Oakley is in hammer-dressed stone and very Gothic, with its asymmetric plan, steep gables, church-like porch and two-centred arches above the windows. Laurel Bank is a handsome neo-classical house in hammer-dressed stone with prominent quoins and an Ionic-columned porch. Only in the last case is an architect, John Eastwood, identified.[135] However, Kirk added a new wing to Oakley House in 1882 and out-buildings to Hungerford House in 1888. Edward Brooke also chose to add a coachman's cottage and stables to Oakley in 1874 but, with Laurel Bank already next door, these were

Fig.65
Laurel Bank, Hungerford Rd and its stairwell bay window.

built on an empty plot beyond it, and the brick-built cottage, much altered, survives today as **Granville (26)**, the last building on the left. Its modest if faintly Gothic appearance notwithstanding, this was by a substantial Leeds architect, Charles Fowler, who was much engaged at the time with

Huddersfield Board Schools, including Mount Pleasant, Lockwood with its notable tower.[136] Interestingly the cottage retained its function into the mid-20th century, becoming home to the chauffeurs of residents of The Gables, Thornhill Rd (see p.109).

Across the road are two substantial Italianate houses. The upper one, **Somerville (27)** (listed II; also gate piers), was built for the pharmacist Robert Fell around 1863 and he remained until his death aged 86 in 1910, describing himself in the 1901 Census as a lead manufacturer. It is pleasingly asymmetric in plan and with impressively rich carved decoration of Renaissance or Baroque origin, particularly in the porch. When Huddersfield Parish Church vestry began, in 1860, to elect a 'people's churchwarden', to serve alongside the one appointed by the vicar, Fell was the first man elected to the post.[137]

Next door **Oakwood (28)** (listed II; also gate piers) is substantially larger and equally Italianate but less lavishly decorated (see pp.38–9) for historic pictures of Oakwood). Fronting to Hungerford Rd, it rears up impressively above Halifax Rd with a fine woodland garden, once enlivened by yet another small stream and now providing an adventurous play area for a children's nursery. Inside there is a full-height top-lit hall with bright floor tiles, an elaborate wooden staircase and a fine plaster ceiling. This was home to lawyer John Freeman from 1863 (when he moved from Edgerton Bank) until his death in 1875, and then to his son, Col Charles Freeman JP, also a solicitor, until 1927. John Freeman was involved in public affairs as a member – and briefly chairman – of the Huddersfield Improvement Commissioners and local solicitor to the London & North Western Railway, which operated the Manchester-Leeds route through Huddersfield. Charles was a sportsman, a colonel in the volunteers, a Conservative Party agent and registrar of the county court from 1896.

Looking across the garden of Oakwood from Hungerford Rd, one can appreciate the texture of the Thornhill development. Beyond Oakwood are glimpses of Cote Royd in Halifax Rd, Ravensdeane in Thornhill Rd and other houses, forming a triangle of villas set spaciously in woodland with little reference to the street plan.

Fig.66
Somerville, Hungerford Rd with its richly carved doorcase.

Fig.67
Cote Royd, Halifax Rd, heraldic
motif above the porch and
internal doorway.

Back on the main road, **Cote Royd (29)** (listed II; also gate piers and lamp post), built in 1861/2, is unusual amongst the house names in preserving a memory of the area's rural past; the Lindley Enclosure Award of 1798 depicts "several ancient inclosures ... called the Coat Royds", owned by Thomas Thornhill.[138] The domestic Gothic house was originally home to Wright Mellor. The billiard room, added in 1870 by Paul Robinson of Manchester, is the earliest of the wave and the stables were extended by John Kirk in 1874.

Mellor was one of Edgerton's most significant public figures. From a small business background at Salendine Nook, and with only elementary education, he inherited a flock dealership from his father and then (like Thomas Hirst) 'married well', to Harriet, daughter of the substantial

Fig.68
Trafford House (top) and
Ashleigh, Halifax Rd.

merchant Thomas Kilner, whose business he took over before the latter's death in 1858. (Kilner's own home was Carr House, the handsome town centre Georgian house now incorporated into the Media Centre.) In 1867 he was president of the Chamber of Commerce. By that time, however, already an elected Improvement Commissioner, Mellor – like Edward Brooke at Oakley – was finding public life more interesting than business. A leading Congregationalist, freemason and Liberal, he joined the new Corporation in 1868 and was four times Mayor in the 1870s and 1880s, chairman of the waterworks committee for 20 years, and elected a freeman of the borough in 1889. A JP from 1863, he served also as poor law Guardian, Savings Bank director, Infirmary trustee, School Board member and governor of the Technical College – a model public service career. He sold the business in 1873 but left a personal estate of around £80,000.[139] Occupants after Mellor's death in 1893 were William Firth JP by 1900 and stockbroker William Wimpenny by 1910.

Next along are **Ashleigh & Trafford House (30)** (listed II; also gate piers and lamp post). Elegantly neo-classical and faced in ashlar, with Tuscan porches, these were planned as detached double-fronted houses mirroring each other, though Trafford House is a half-bay wider than Ashleigh. They were built for wool merchant partners George Barker and Edward Booth Woodhead, and were under construction in 1862, when the clients and their architect, Ralph Nicholson, were in dispute with contractor John Eastwood, who was removed from the job and sued for compensation.[140] Both houses were later extended and now adjoin at ground floor level.

Woodhead was at Trafford House until his death in 1911 and commissioned several additions and alterations from Ben Stocks. At Ashleigh, Barker was soon succeeded by another leading wool merchant, James Willans, who stayed until about 1893 before moving to Rose Hill, and then by Sydney Brierley, Marsh woollen manufacturer, before he moved to Hazelgrove. The addition of a half-timbered portable billiard and play room in 1901, by the Portable Building Co of Manchester, was followed in 1905 by minor additions by the Hull architect and art historian G Dudley Harbron, who had married into the Brierley family.

Both Willans and Woodhead were pillars of the town's Liberal establishment. Woodhead's brother-in-law was Joseph Woodhead, founder of the *Examiner* and later MP for Spen Valley. Edward, a Quaker, like Mellor scaled back his business activities to concentrate on Corporation work; keenly interested in horticulture, he made a particular contribution as chairman of the Parks Committee from 1901–10. He was a member, and for several years treasurer, of the bowling club at Edgerton Park.[141] James Willans JP, a Congregationalist and founder of Milton Church, was still better connected to the Liberal cause – his sister Emily was mother to the future Liberal prime minister Herbert Asquith, who was brought up in Huddersfield by his Willans grandparents and briefly attended Huddersfield College as a boy. Born in 1842, James Willans was profiled in the *Examiner* in February 1924 as "the Grand Old Man of Huddersfield ... [who] has seen the whole pageant of Victorian England go by." The encomium particularly emphasised his service to education, as a School Board member from 1880 and chair of the Corporation's education committee when they assumed control in 1902; he was also the first chairman of the library and art gallery after its belated establishment in 1898. When he became a freeman of the borough in 1918, schoolchildren were given a half-holiday, "that they might in after years be interested in public service".[142]

By 1911, however, he had been succeeded at Ashleigh by a less sober character – woollen manufacturer Joseph Hilton Crowther. One of the Colne Valley industrial dynasty, and prone to motoring accidents and speeding fines, in 1908 he supplied the finance for the founding of Huddersfield Town FC. He was a director and major financial supporter of the club until 1919, when he proposed a merger with struggling Leeds United. This did not go down well with local fans and he parted company with Town, later becoming chairman at Leeds. Town's new owners recruited the legendary manager Herbert Chapman, who led the club to its glory days as League champions and FA Cup winners in the 1920s.

Mr. J. E. Willans, J.P.

Fig.69
James Willans of Ashleigh.

Thornhill Road and beyond

THORNHILL RD WAS developed a little later than the roads discussed so far, in the main just into the 1870s. Its northern section has half a dozen interesting and varied houses where, as a result, it is usually possible to identify the architects – who are not confined to Huddersfield's 'usual suspects'.

Turning in from the main road, first on the left is the Italianate **Ravensdeane (31)** (listed II; also gate piers and lodge), almost certainly by the leading Bradford architects Lockwood & Mawson (noted for City Hall, Salt's Mill and much more).[143] The three-storey tower and the doorway it contains are particularly fine features, though the aspect is badly obstructed by poor in-fill development. The client was John Taylor, whose father Henry Beaumont Taylor was a drysalter (a supplier of chemicals) at Market St and Rashcliffe – evidently a booming business at the time, as Taylor commissioned Ravensdeane when he was only 25. Sadly, however, he died in 1871 aged 29, leaving a widow and two young children; his parents then moved up from York House, New North Rd to share Ravensdeane with them. Henry remained until his death in 1897, and the house was renamed Clarence Lodge over these years. He took on an additional plot, moved the lodge further up the road, and commissioned outbuildings from John Kirk in 1873 and a house extension from Ben Stocks in 1887. The original occupier, J H Taylor, is commemorated by a window at St Stephen's, Lindley by Ward & Hughes, noted for their work at Lincoln Cathedral.

The Taylors were followed by 1901 by railway contractor Thompson Naylor, who had left by 1913, when his fine collection of china was put up for sale and he moved to Ireland.[144] He was a major civil engineer, whose firm's work included the towering Denby Dale viaduct. The discovery there of a rich seam of clay led to the foundation of a clay brick and pipe factory, which has evolved into the today's Naylor Group of companies.

After Ravensdeane comes **The Gables (32)** of 1889/90, brick-built, tile-hung, with a half-timbered gable, in a 'Norman Shaw' style entirely out of character for the neighbourhood but perhaps refreshingly so. It is a modest house on a large plot, built with only two reception rooms, two principal

Fig.70
Ravensdeane, Thornhill Rd.

bedrooms and a basement billiard room. The architects were Edward Salomons & Alfred Steinthal of Manchester; Salomons is noted for the Manchester Synagogue and Reform Club and worked with Huddersfield architect W H Crossland on his master-work, Royal Holloway College at Egham, Surrey. They must presumably have been known to the client, the exotically named Camille Bernard Knight, a shipping agent based in Dundas St and trading mainly with the USA (where he was born) – but seem to have found Huddersfield Corporation's building regulations irksome. The Borough Surveyor required larger flues than they intended, prompting this rebuke:

> It seems to us a most extraordinary thing that a gentleman cannot be allowed to build a house as he likes as long as he does not interfere with his neighbours. If a chimney smokes he is the only sufferer. We have been 35 years in practice building first class property and have

Fig.71
The Gables, Thornhill Rd.

come to the conclusion that a 9" by 9" flue for a private house is the best safe-guard against the smoking of chimnies [sic] and we are not allowed to profit by our experience.[145]

Knight's successor by 1901 was woollen manufacturer Edward Bruce JP, who remained until his death in June 1931. Son of the renowned Congregationalist minister Dr Robert Bruce, of Highfield Chapel (but an Anglican himself, and a Liberal), he headed the woollen manufacturers, Crowther, Bruce & Co of Marsden and left £149,000, including a small legacy to set up a trust for the poor of Marsden. His extensive musical and artistic interests included "one of the finest collections of Chinese brasses in the country".[146]

Crossing to the opposite side of Thornhill Rd and walking back downhill, next are **Burbank** & **Fernleigh (33)** (listed II, also gate piers of Burbank), a pair of large semis of somewhat stolid form but enlivened with varied

Fig.72
Burbank (left() and Fernleigh,
Thornhill Rd.

Gothic details and an observation tower – "a most unusual room ... which provides a flood of natural light and allows views through the adjacent wooded area", to quote 1998 sale particulars. These were built in the mid-1870s for John Liddell, a partner in Liddell & Brierley of Marsh, woollen manufacturers and a Territorial Army officer; he moved into Burbank himself around 1890 and was there at least until 1914.[147] His father Joseph had been in partnership with Pat Martin (see p.45) in earlier times, and Fernleigh was Martin's last home before his death in 1882. After him came William Whiteley, machine-maker, who moved on to The Knowle, and by 1910 engineer Percy Holmes, of gas equipment makers W C Holmes, who later commissioned Low Wood (see p.118). Today Fernleigh has been renamed Thornleigh (duplicating a name in Bryan Rd, p.122).

Next down, across Dingley Rd, is **Buckden Mount (34)** (listed II; also gate piers), with a "picturesque plan of some complexity", to quote the listing. Its round-headed arches, massively overhanging eaves and delicate cast-iron

Fig.73
Buckden Mount, Thornhill Rd.

loggia offer the best local examples of these Italianate details. The house was built in 1872 for Frederick Eastwood, a worsted manufacturer with mills at Engine Bridge, at the bottom of Chapel Hill, where his grandfather John had established a dyeworks early in the 19th century. The original Building Plan is missing but, from those for the extensions to the stabling in 1876, and to the house in 1880 – the three-storey portion facing Dingley Rd – it seems certain that Eastwood had turned to his brother-in-law Thomas Healey.[148] He and his brother Francis were established Bradford architects, noted particularly for their Gothic churches there and, in Huddersfield, for the former Milton (Congregational) Church on Queensgate. Eastwood was a substantial public figure – a JP, treasurer to the Infirmary from 1875, President of the Chamber of Commerce in 1896 – and a deacon in the Congregationalist church. After his death in 1911, the house remained in the family until 1921.

Thorn Hill (35) (listed II) also remained in its orginal client's occupation well into the 20th century. It was built in 1875 on Thornhill Rd for the Thornhill estate agent George Henry Crowther, who lived there until his death in 1913 – and who was unlikely to forget where his loyalties lay! With his son Fred and the waterworks engineers Thomas and Charles Hawksley, he designed the Huddersfield Corporation waterworks. Thorn Hill's well-executed Gothic design, with good variety of detail around a basic symmetry of plan, and an excellent doorway, was the work of Edward Hughes.[149] Now a care home, it has been much extended.

The last house before the main road, opposite Ravensdeane, is **Springfield (36)** (listed II; also gate piers). Another Italianate house, but from about 1863, this is much more in the mould of Oakwood and Somerville than its later and sprightlier neighbour Buckden Mount. The exterior decorative work earns one of the longest of the listing entries, which also comments on the "lavish plasterwork [and] elaborate staircase with very rich turned wooden balusters". It was built for one of the wealthiest of the wool merchants, David Midgley, whose probate valuation in 1894 was £127,821,[150] and remained in the family until 1915. The son of an Almondbury grocer, Midgley had built up a large trading business in Huddersfield, Bradford

Fig.74
Springfield, Thornhill Rd.

and Manchester. Like many successful businessmen, his apprenticeship had
been in the offices of Frederick Schwann, another of the town's German
merchants, and like several of Schwann's protégés he was a supporter of
the Mechanics' Institute. He was a JP, a long-time Council member of
the Chamber of Commerce, and a Free Wesleyan at Brunswick St chapel.
Like his neighbour H B Taylor at Ravensdeane, he commemorated his son
Edward, who died young, in a window at St Stephen's, Lindley – this one
destroyed by a bomb blast in World War II.

Beyond Thornhill Rd, as Edgerton shades into Lindley, the land remained
undeveloped until the very end of the 19th century, when two mansions,
Banney Royd and Norwood, were built on a grander scale than anything
encountered so far. These were discussed above (p.66) and lie beyond this
itinerary. But the Thornhill land to the east of Halifax Rd, which we left at
Glenwood, now requires attention.

Edgerton Park & Kaffir Road

OPPOSITE THE HOUSES on Halifax Rd, from Willow Bank to Cote Royd,
is the open space, now much overgrown, of Edgerton Park, the origins of
which were described above (p.34). Its atmosphere in its heyday is evoked
in a memoir of an Edwardian childhood spent in Imperial Rd:

> There were two tennis courts, one at either end, and a beautiful
> bowling green where Daddy tried his skill at every opportunity. The
> park played a large part in our youth and there we learned to play
> tennis. We had picnic teas on the slanting lawn, maddened by the
> relentless midges. We tried everything, oils and lotions and scents,
> begging anyone to smoke to gain relief ... I have never experienced
> anywhere else such persistent waves of these small insects.[151]

The tennis courts "languished" after World War I but remained until
World War II, while the bowling club survived until 1957, according to
an *Examiner* report that year, which also mentioned that it had once been
graced by "some interesting pieces of ivy-mantled statuary".[152]

Behind the Park are the houses of Kaffir Rd, mainly built by chemical pioneer Read Holliday (see p.67). His own home, **Lunnclough Hall (37)** (listed II; also gate piers and lodge), dates from 1855 and is accessed by a private drive from the right-angled corner in Kaffir Rd (below Glenwood) – he leased extra land to enclose what the estate had first planned as Forester Rd – and its romantic description in 1860 was quoted above (p.41). More prosaically, this is a Tudor Gothic house designed by Pritchett & Sons, most probably James Pigott Pritchett himself, and substantially extended by Willie Cooper in 1889 for Holliday's eldest son Thomas.[153] Down the drive, only the porte-cochere (carriage porch) can be glimpsed without trespassing; probably the only one in Huddersfield, it has much in common with other work by Pritchett, including Huddersfield College in New North Rd. A better idea of the house as a whole can be had from Sunny Side (p.93).

Although richly Gothic in its details, the house was designed symmetrically around a top-lit circular hall – a most unusual plan – and capped by a 60-foot 'campanile'. At the top, the 1860 sale particulars relate, was an observatory

Fig.75
Lunnclough Hall, Kaffir Rd: the rear elevation (above) and front elevation (below).

FRONT ELEVATION

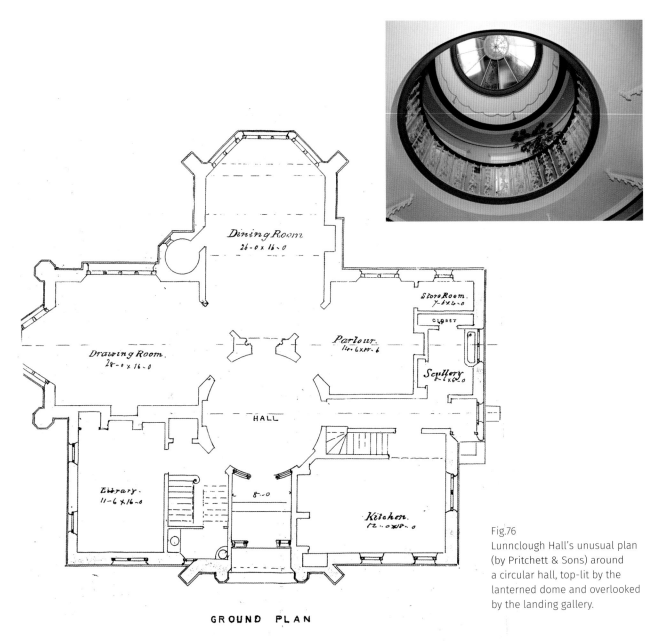

GROUND PLAN

Fig.76
Lunnclough Hall's unusual plan
(by Pritchett & Sons) around
a circular hall, top-lit by the
lanterned dome and overlooked
by the landing gallery.

Fig.77
'Battle of the styles' in Kaffir Rd: Hollinhurst & Holmwood, Woodlands and Oakleigh (top to bottom).

where "Six people can sit ... comfortably. Gentlemen fond of the weed can enjoy themselves to perfection in this airy region. Four of the windows open for the purpose of using telescopes." The house was not sold then – it was only five years old, and only marketed by Read Holliday as part of a threat to quit the town, during a dispute with the Improvement Commissioners about pollution from his Turnbridge works. In fact the last Holliday of the house, Thomas's widow Maria, was there until she died in 1936. Today it is divided into two homes.

As mentioned earlier, Holliday turned property developer and had houses built on the next two plots along Kaffir Rd in the 1860s. First (Nos. 12 & 14) are the large neo-classical ashlar semis, **Hollinhurst** & **Holmwood** (38) (listed II; also gate piers), forming a right-angled pair of interlocked L-shaped plans. The unusual attic windows were no doubt servants' quarters but Holmwood also acquired a narrow added service wing at some point. To the rear the houses have a spectacular setting above a glen, formed by a stream once feeding into Sunny Bank Beck and now culverted.

Holmwood was occupied by 1868 by William England, a chemist and druggist in Market Place, who moved up from Bay Hall and named the house Bythewood Hollow. He was an early Improvement Commissioner, Infirmary Governor and a churchwarden until his marriage to a Unitarian, after which he joined that denomination and became a founding trustee of Fitzwilliam St chapel. Around 1880 the house passed to barrister William Johnson Kaye JP, son-in-law of George Henry Brook at Edgerton Cottage, and in 1901 to civil engineer John Hanson. Hollinhurst was home to Rachel Hirst from 1875 to 1890, followed by Frederick Sykes, son of William (see p.82), and woollen buyer John Exley by 1911.

Next (No. 16) is **Woodlands** (39) (listed II; also gate piers), a well-composed Italianate house of 1868 with a three-storey tower to rival that at Bremen House. An early tenant was another druggist, Fredrick Langton, followed in the mid-1870s by William

Moore, a sharebroker and 'Church' School Board member, who remained there until his death in 1907. His father, also William, was Huddersfield postmaster from 1832–61 and was a combative and cantankerous Whig in the turbulent politics of that period.[154] (Glen Garth, No 18, is a more recent addition.)

After the Holliday houses come **Oakleigh (40)** (Nos. 20/22) & (facing the road) **Brantwood (No 24)**, formerly Woodbine (both listed II; also gate piers). Once again right-angled semis, of disparate size, these are a medley of Gothic and Italianate features, most noticeable among which are the elaborately bargeboarded gables, eaves and porches – Oakleigh's including a trio of columns with disparate capitals, said to embody Masonic symbolism. They were built around 1866 as an investment by James Burman, a decorator and wallpaper merchant, who lived at Woodbine until 1879. Oakleigh was first let to Frederick Learoyd, another of the 'Leeds Rd' Learoyds, who switched from wool to cotton spinning. In the mid-1870s he was replaced by the aptly-named shoddy manufacturer (and churchwarden) John Grist, Burman's son-in-law; he came to lease the whole plot, extending to the corner of Bryan Rd. Grist's daughters ran a school there from 1885 to 1900. Early C20 occupants were paper manufacturer Ben Haigh JP – who left a fortune of around £80,000 in 1906 – and draper Thomas Mellor. At Brantwood, meanwhile, manufacturing chemist George Hoerle (of Robinson & Co at Hillhouse), and in due course his widow, were the tenants from the 1880s. A century later, in 1988, the house featured as the home of Deborah Norbury in several episodes of the BBC's 'First of the Summer Wine', a prequel to the famous Holmfirth-based series.

The westerly part of Grist's plot is now occupied by two Arts & Crafts houses of 1924–6, **Bryan Croft (41)** and **Low Wood (42)**, not unlike several others around Huddersfield but unusual here in being inserted amid the Victorian villas. Both were designed with service rooms and servant quarters. Bryan Croft is by Oswald White, whose own house, Hope Garth, is nearby on Halifax Rd. Low Wood (originally Coverdale), was badly damaged by fire in 2016. Its interesting butterfly-plan design was by Calvert & Jessop of Nottingham, who also worked on the Portland St buildings of

Fig.78
Bryan Rd looking north, with the lodge of Woodleigh on the left in the early 20th century.

118

Fig.79
The Grange, Halifax Rd.

Huddersfield Royal Infirmary with local architect Joseph Berry. The client, gas equipment manufacturer Percy Holmes, was a cousin of Charles Calvert and an Infirmary Board member – one of several examples where family connections brought out-of-town architects to Huddersfield. A famous 20th century resident was 'four-minute miler' Derek Ibbotson.

Bryan Road, Binham Road & Rose Hill

TURNING THE CORNER into Bryan Rd, one crosses yet another ravine, now dry. Rearing above it to the left is **The Grange** (43) (see p.119) and its restored terrace gardens, which make dramatic use of the site. Whilst this villa fronts onto Halifax Rd, the view from Bryan Rd (fig.79) is much better than can be had from the main road. It is a Gothic pile of about 1860 with Venetian details, taking full advantage of a steep fall to the beck below to emphasise its grandeur. The 2007 Conservation Area review particularly compliments it on its scalloped roof slates, decorative timber barge boards and crested ridge; the lodge is excellent too. This was home to Joseph Lowenthal, another German wool merchant (arriving in England in 1839 aged 21), who served on the Chamber of Commerce and as a JP and technical college governor. But the Lowenthal name is perhaps better remembered now for his daughter Bertha, one of Joseph's seven children and a suffragette celebrated in Jill Liddington's book *Rebel Girls*.[155] Joseph died in 1903 but his son Charles was there until 1928; a leading lawyer, in 1919 he became the first Recorder of Huddersfield when local Quarter Sessions began.

Fig.80
Bryan Wood, Bryan Rd.

Beyond the glen is the additional Thornhill land purchase of 1858 (see p.28), on which the estate secured the most spacious and secluded part of the entire development – though with honourable exceptions the architects did not rise to the challenge, and few houses here are listed.

Taking the right hand side of the road, the first house is **Bryan Wood** (**44**) (originally Brooklyn), built in 1862/3, with three reception rooms and eight bedrooms, for the portrait painter and musician Samuel Howell when he moved up from Bath Buildings. Originally from Knaresborough, he settled in Huddersfield after his artistic training in London and specialised in portraits of the wealthy gentlemen of the neighbourhood; no fewer than nine of these are now owned by public galleries, including several in the Kirklees collection.[156] Howell was also a musician, playing the violin or cello, and was President of Huddersfield Choral Society, while two of his daughters were accomplished sopranos who sang with local choirs; it is perhaps no surprise that another subject of his portraits, now hanging in the Town Hall, is of Mrs Sunderland, the 'Yorkshire Queen of Song'.

In a stolid Italianate style with none of the appealing asymmetry of Oakwood or Buckden Mount, the house has distinctive dormer windows – perhaps lighting the artist's studio, or they may be later additions. After Howell's death in 1876, his wife and daughters continued to occupy the house until the mid-1890s. In the 20th century it was home to the Whitfield family, of the local department store; the actress June Whitfield was a relation of theirs. Subsequently it was divided, with an awkward outside staircase leading to first floor accommodation named 'Woodside', and its modern use as a care home has brought a large modern extension to the rear.

Following the curve into Binham Rd, one comes next to **Cedar Grove** (**45**) on the left, latterly The Mount School. Another uninspired Italianate house, this was designed by John Kirk in 1869 for Ephraim Beaumont Taylor, woollen manufacturer, whose monogram is to be found in the glass of the inner front door. He and his son Stanley had the house until 1908, when it was taken for 40 years by W E Rippon, of the famous Huddersfield coach-building business, who would no doubt have supplied his neighbours with the coachwork of their luxury cars. Across the way the lodge, also by

Fig.81
Ephraim Beaumont Taylor's monogram at Cedar Mount, Binham Rd.

Kirk, was intended to accompany a second villa, but only now is a house being built there!

Binham Rd now peters out, but the 1852 Tolson plan for this area (see p.33) promised that it could be approached either from Halifax Rd or by a carriage drive leading up from Lea Head, below today's Spink's Nest pub is on Blacker Rd. As noted above (p.91), this also gave secluded access to Hazelgrove on Edgerton Rd. It survived as a narrow footpath continuing from Binham Rd until the 1990s, but the fencing of St Patrick's School grounds has closed this route. However Cedar Grove commands an attractive view down the valley.

Returning towards Bryan Rd, on the right are the semis of **Thornleigh** & **Binham Lodge (46)**, now combined. Like the previous two houses, these are Italianate and unlisted – perhaps all products of Kirk's burst of activity in the early 1860s (see p.43). They were built for solicitor Charles Mills, who lived at Thornleigh until his death in 1919. John Brook records that Mills was a brilliant scholar in his youth, fluent in several languages, who became Clerk to the Justices and Advisory Secretary of the Chamber of Commerce. In the latter capacity, he wrote most of the articles in a multi-lingual year book, published by the Chamber in 1918 to promote Huddersfield business overseas.[157] Binham Lodge was first occupied by George Pesel, a merchant connected with Thomas Varley (Edgerton House) and a cousin of Frederick Schwann, who shot himself in 1880 aged 42. He was followed by another of the German merchants, Henry Anders (moving up from The Mount) and then a Scottish woollen manufacturer, John Stewart. Colourful 20th century occupants were the Cumming Bell family. Ann Cumming Bell married the Duke of Rutland in 1946, in a ceremony with huge crowds at St Margaret's, Westminster.[158] The marriage broke down by 1953; shortly thereafter her father, Major Cumming Bell (of W. E. Wimpenny & Co, Huddersfield stockbrokers) was found shot through the head in his bedroom there,[159] after which the house was put on the market, 'suitable for conversion to flats'.

Beyond this on the right of Bryan Rd are modern houses which show little respect for the setting. Starting again from the ravine, on the left hand

Fig.82
Thornleigh & Binham Lodge,
Bryan Rd.

Fig.83
Woodleigh, Bryan Rd.

side opposite Bryanwood is **Woodleigh (47)**, built as another plain pair of Italianate semis in the early 1860s, though with splendid surviving interiors (fig.84), and again unlisted. For a while the left-hand house was renamed Bryan Lodge, becoming a Corporation aged persons' home in 1952, but they are now united as Alwoodleigh care home. They were built for solicitor Thomas Brook, who occupied Bryan Lodge himself; after his death in 1876 he was followed by Charles Ingram Armitage (of the Armitage clan, see p.46) until 1885, and then by woollen merchant Edward Fisher, who bought the freehold of both houses in 1889.[160] Fisher funded scholarships for Huddersfield area commercial students to live abroad for a year, to support them in "perfecting their knowledge of foreign languages and acquiring an insight into the commercial methods of those countries".[161] Meanwhile Woodleigh was home to wool spinner Ludlam Ramsden; then to George Knight, father of C B Knight at The Gables; and, from 1882 until his death in 1912, to the 'black dyer' Frederick Robinson.[162]

Fig.84
The morning room at Bryan Lodge, Bryan Rd.

Fig.85
Oakfield Lodge, Bryan Rd.

After these come three houses of about 1860. **Oakfield Lodge (48)** is essentially another Italianate house, but attractively asymmetric and with Gothic details, including a tourelle (corner tower) with capped roof and a thrusting porch. For many years this was home to the Huths. One of the German wool merchants, Edward Huth JP had settled in the town around 1840 and "threw himself heart and soul into the work of the Huddersfield Mechanics' Institute and its more important successor, the Technical College", where his portrait hung from 1888.[163] His wife Marion was equally interested in education and was elected to the School Board from its inception in 1871 – a rare instance at that date of a woman active in public life (though she was debarred from voting!). Husband and wife together were "the driving force in the Female Educational Institute".[164] Marion Huth was also a practitioner of sign language for deaf mutes, who made a presentation to her in 1890 for her work on their behalf.[165] Edward Huth died in 1892 and the house came to market in 1895. The freehold was acquired by Henry Martin of Stoneleigh (see p.127) and by 1899 the house was occupied by Edward William Fisher, son of Edward Fisher across the road at Bryan Lodge and newly married in 1898 to Blanche Martin, Henry's daughter. A woollen merchant like his father, he died aged 54 in 1928 a year after buying a 12,000 acre estate at Malham Tarn for £28,000, including a mansion, the Tarn itself and sporting rights. He also owned a freehold house in Bournemouth and left "all his cars" to his widow; his total estate was about £367,000.[166]

Next is **Beechwood (49)** (listed II; also gate piers and gate), a tidy neo-classical house, if undistinguished beyond the facade; it was built for James Watkinson, who founded the business of that name at Washpit Mills above Holmfirth, and extended in 1889 by Ben Stocks. Watkinson moved up from New North Rd and was followed after his death in 1874 by cotton spinner John Marsden JP, but Watkinson's son Thomas was there in the 1890s, and Horace Martin JP – son of Henry next door at Stoneleigh – from about 1900. A care home for disabled adults since 1966, the house has attractive gardens with a large square pond, recently restored. In the late C19 they provided the setting for grand weddings, for example in July 1899 when 250 guests celebrated the marriage of Agnes Watkinson to neighbour Frederick Robinson JP of Woodleigh.[167] Coming within months of the Fisher/Martin marriage next door, this emphasises what an enclave of inter-married opulence Bryan Rd had become.

Last in the road, by then at the heart of this commercial and social nexus, and perhaps in its prime the best of the Edgerton houses, is **Stoneleigh (50)** (listed II). Featured in George Sheeran's *Brass Castles*, it was built in 1860 for cigar maker Edward Beaumont. He and his older brother Joseph, who rented Greenhead Hall, were employing some 50 men at their works in Fitzwilliam St at that time. But the business depended on imports from the plantations of their slave-owning uncles in Tennessee, and the disruption caused by the American Civil War may have led to Edward's putting the new mansion on the market in 1865, when it was bought by the woollen manufacturer Samuel Turner Learoyd.[168]

Fig.86
Stoneleigh, Bryan Rd. To the right are modern garage additions and to the left a glimpse in the background of the modern Stoneleigh Pavilions.

Fig.87
Details from Stoneleigh's
entrance tower.

The original house is in a free Gothic style, quite Flemish in character but with varied English motifs, arranged asymmetrically around a thrusting porch beneath a three-storcy spired tower, and with a (much-altered) service wing to the right; the architect is sadly unknown. The elephant and castle motif on the tower is interpreted by Sheeran as "a symbol, perhaps, of business sagacity and perseverance".[169] Stoneleigh passed from Learoyd to Henry Martin of Wellington Mills by 1884 and he began to commission additions to the house. After Henry's death in 1910, his eldest son Horace extended it further, moving from Beechwood in 1911. Most of the additions were designed by the Wellington Mills millwright Edmund Bamford or his son Dennis, who described himself as an 'architect', aged 17, in the 1901 Census and went on to serve his articles with Edgar Wood and London architect Beresford Pite en route to his RIBA qualifications. Between them, from 1884 to 1911, the Bamfords twice extended the service range – 18 staff were employed there in the late C19 – and added extensive garden buildings across the road (on an extra plot bought by Beaumont and now occupied by modern housing). An attached domed orangery was also added during this period, perhaps by Ben Stocks.[170]

More importantly, however, in 1889 Henry Martin bought the freehold and commissioned a large rear extension from George Faulkner Armitage of Altrincham.[171] He was a leading figure in the Arts & Crafts movement in the North, sometimes likened to William Morris and holding the Manchester agency for Morris & Co. One historian has written that Armitage's chief work "lay in furnishing the bedrooms, bathrooms, billiard rooms and drawing-rooms of the Forsytes of provincial England".[172] Other Huddersfield clients included James Willans (probably at Rose Hill, see p.131), J H Kaye (probably at Hazelgrove), Thomas Edward Hirst at Willow Bank (see p.99) and the Corporation, for whom Armitage provided decoration for the first public library in Byram St. At Stoneleigh he created an immense billiard-cum-ballroom, 46' x 39': coats of arms of 24 Yorkshire towns in the plaster frieze, stained glass panels behind seats and a pierced gilded ceiling made this "an interior of more than ordinary quality".[173] Above were three bedrooms; the external treatment was a plainer Tudor Gothic than the original but roofed with matching 'Flemish' gables.

Martin was evidently proud of his patronage, commissioning the leading architectural photographers Bedford Lemere & Co to prepare an album showing the new wing.[174] This also shows that several rooms in the original house had been extravagantly remodelled, probably in 1889, by leading Leeds furniture makers Marsh, Jones & Cribb, whose principal designer was the celebrated Art & Crafts architect W R Lethaby. Both they and Faulkner Armitage had exhibited at the 1883 Huddersfield Fine Art & Industrial Exhibition, perhaps bringing them to the attention of wealthy local clients.

Henry Martin also substantially extended and landscaped the grounds behind the house at some point between 1893 and 1907, introducing a fountain – reputedly Huddersfield's tallest – and incorporating a farm, Stamil Royd, as out-buildings, including a stables block. It was another Dennis Bamford project, in 1911, to convert this as a top-lit motor garage with inspection pits.[175] These developments completed the conversion of the 'triangle of opulence' referred to above (p.67) from agricultural use to high quality residential estates.

But Stoneleigh continued to evolve in the C20. The celebrated 1890 wing had been demolished, in unknown circumstances, by 1949, when Huddersfield Corporation bought the house for conversion to a 23-bed local authority care home.[176] Its site was first occupied by a large conservatory, with a replacement billiard room replacing first-floor service accommodation; presumably inter-war occupiers, Feeneys in the 1920s or Kayes in the 1930s, must have been responsible for these changes. In turn the conservatory was replaced by extended but disappointingly designed local authority accommodation, now further modified to 'Stoneleigh Mews', comprising six flats, with the original house divided into seven more. The unashamedly modern Stoneleigh Pavilions by Aedas (Abbey Hanson Rowe), another block of flats carefully sited among trees at the rear of the grounds, is a much happier addition to the site.

Across from Stoneleigh is a small Tudor lodge described in the 1871 Census as 'Thornhill's Lodge' and occupied by a farm labourer, housekeeper

Fig.88
Stoneleigh. Top: new 1889 wing from the south-west, and its billiard room interior, by George Faulkner Armitage. Bottom: interiors by Marsh, Jones & Cribb, also probably of 1889, in the original house.

Fig.89
Stoneleigh from the SE (top right), some years after the 1889 extension; the service staff in the Martin era; the bothy, with gardening staff; and a senior gardener in the greenhouses across Bryan Rd.

and scholar. Whether this originally served as a gatehouse for Bryan Rd as a whole is unclear, though we know the Thornhill's planned development at Calverley had several entrance lodges. However, by the late C19 it was incorporated into the Stoneleigh estate as the bothy (fig.89).

Passing the lodge and turning right into Birkby Rd, after about 100 metres one reaches the entrance to **Rose Hill (51)** (listed II*), though it is necessary to go a little further to catch a glimpse of the house. This would now be classed as Birkby rather than Edgerton, but its affinity is with its Bryan Rd neighbours rather than the C20 housing now occupying most of its grounds. In origin it is a late Georgian house; not shown on the '1780' Ramsden map (fig.4) but certainly standing by 1828, when it was purchased by wool merchant Jeremiah Riley. The business partner and son-in-law of Joseph Brook of Greenhead (see p.48), Riley was the patron who had brought the artist Samuel Howell of Bryan Wood (p.121) to Huddersfield.[177] Despite Brook's business crash, Riley's fortune on his death in 1865 ran into millions in today's values and included a house in Royal Crescent, Bath, where he had retired months beforehand in an attempt to maintain his health.

Rose Hill was retained by Riley's trustees until 1890 and let out successively to millowner Joshua Schofield in 1865, woollen manufacturer Godfrey Berry Crowther in 1877, and then to his widow Rosalina and her second husband, cotton broker Robert Cameron (it appears that Crowther moved there from Hazelgrove, just across the valley, and that the Camerons returned there!). It came to auction in 1890, after Mrs Riley's death in 1887, and was sold to John Martin; later occupiers were wool merchant James Willans by 1893 (moving from Ashleigh) and Joe Lumb, owner of Folly Hall Mills, by 1909, with Willans moving to Bremen House. Neither Victorian nor strictly Edgerton, Rose Hill was evidently well integrated into the continual movements between the Edgerton villas.

Like its neighbours in the 'triangle of opulence', it also evidenced Huddersfield's fin-de-siecle patronage of fashionable design and architecture. Willans was a customer of Faulkner Armitage, commissioning fittings and furniture in 1893, probably for Rose Hill, while Lumb was the client for 1909 interiors by Edgar Wood and J H Sellers, extravagantly described in the list description as comparing well with Joseph Hoffmann's Palais Stoclet (1905) and Alfred Loos' Kartner Bar in Vienna (1907), which are celebrated in every account of Art Nouveau and its passage to modernism. These rooms appear as the setting of a party in James Mason's 1972 ITV film 'Home James', which also describes Stoneleigh and neighbouring properties as 'some of the grander Victorian mansions'.

It remains to visit the houses built on Fenton land in 'lower Edgerton' to form Queen's Rd and Murray Rd. This can be achieved by retracing steps along Bryan Rd and the main road, perhaps taking in houses not viewed on the outward journey. Alternatively, one can take a more direct route via a narrow ginnel next to the Bryan Rd lodge. Once known locally as 'spider alley', this proceeds for several hundred metres between high walls, which conceal the houses of Bryan and Binham Roads to the right and the Rose Hill estate to the left, now host to the natural burial ground. Turning right at the first opportunity (by St Patrick's School), one can then cross Clayton Dike at a footbridge and climb alongside Waverley (Hazelgrove) to rejoin Edgerton Rd by the tram shelter. Alternatively, one can turn left after the bridge and – at least for now – pick one's way across Clayton Fields to Queen's Rd. It is hoped that the planned housing development there will maintain this permissive route.

Queen's Road & Murray Road

QUEEN'S RD LEAVES Edgerton Rd between two houses described above (p.82), Burleigh and Bremen House. Beyond Burleigh/Elm Crest on the left are **Springfield & Bankfield (52)**, yet another pair of substantial Italianate semis by John Kirk & Sons; they are set at right-angles, and Bankfield is considerably larger. Springfield's incised segmented lintel, reminiscent of Oak Lea (p.87), contrasts nicely with Bankfield's canted bay; behind, the fall of the land affords an elevated view across Clayton Fields. The original lease for both was taken out by woollen merchant William Nield, and his children's names can still be seen scratched into several windows of

Fig.90
Springfield, Queen's Rd.

Bankfield, though this was soon let to Charles Wheatley, a drugs merchant, whose son William remained at least until 1911. By 1877 Springfield was let to Ambrose Moorhouse, a woollen manufacturer, and by 1911 Joseph Wheatley was there, brother to William next door.

The next two plots offered for lease by the Fentons were not built on until the late 1960s, when they became the site of Deveron Grove. The first of these, adjacent to his own home, was also leased by Charles Wheatley, and used as a smallholding producing vegetables and chickens,[178] and the next was taken by Thomas Kaye, but also not built on. Then comes **Deveron House (53)**, a plain classical house of 1906 with some Arts & Crafts detailing in its tall chimneys and unusual brackets atop the bays. This was designed by Willie Cooper for yarn spinner John Stork, who was there until 1911, when the house appears simply as 'New House' in the Census. Later on it was home to Arthur Longden Woodhead, managing director of the *Examiner*. The unusual name 'Deveron' is taken from a Scottish salmon river which was, and still is, very popular with local fishermen, and there is a Scottish feel about several of the house names hereabouts.

Next is **Burnieside (54)**, generally a bland house externally (and with no plan found to identify the architect) but enlivened by a pillared entrance porch below a conical-capped tower. Built in the 1880s – coming to market a few years after the other landowners, the Fenton estate seem to have taken longer to find takers for their plots – this was built for Thomas Kaye, linen draper and silk mercer and passed by 1911 to woollen manufacturer George Crowther Hirst.

Following the curve round, next door is **Sedgefield (55)** (listed II; also gate piers), built in the early 1870s for woollen manufacturer Livingston Middlemost – whose monogram it displays – and probably designed by Kirk.[179] The Gothic design here makes effective use of a range of motifs, including Caernarvon-arched windows, hoodmoulds and a crenellated parapet, to enliven its L-shaped plan. Middlemost moved there from Oak Villa at the top of New North Rd; his daughter Lucy's wedding in 1895 to Shepley woollen manufacturer Richard Barnicot brought a "large and fashionable assembly"[180] to Holy Trinity; and a Middlemost was still in

Fig.91
Deveron House, Queen's Rd.

residence in 1911. The name survives in Middlemost Pond above Norman Park, Birkby – a mill dam for the former Clough House Mills, which were owned by Middlemost Bros from 1895 until their closure in 1971.[181] The house faces onto one of two triangular road islands, much like those at Bryan Rd but rather better maintained, as they were sold to the Corporation in 1912.[182]

Continuing on the left, next are **Holly Bank & Westoe (56)**, symmetrical semis with a bargeboarded double porch. The leasehold developers here were builders Joseph & William Radcliffe and the architect perhaps J H Abbey.[183] The Radcliffes sold the lease to woollen merchant John Beaumont, an Anglican member of the School Board, who occupied Holly Bank himself until his death in 1913. At Westoe Martha Lancaster, widow of the well-known local auctioneer John Lancaster, was in residence by 1881, followed by 1891 by the accountant George Pepler Norton. He and his partner

Fig.92
Sedgefield, Queen's Rd.

W H Armitage JP were further patrons of contemporary architecture. Norton moved on to Birkby Lodge, where he commissioned Edgar Wood and his partner J H Sellers to undertake alterations and extensions, and later to High Royd, Honley, where Sellers undertook an interior for him. Meanwhile Armitage, briefly a Queen's Rd neighbour at Storalee (see below), went one further by commissioning Banney Royd (see p.66) from Wood. Their careers illustrate how Huddersfield's industrial and commercial wealth spilled over into indispensable and lucrative ancillary professions such as accountancy.

Beyond these houses, and almost completely obscured by vegetation, is **Elmford (57)**, built for wool merchant Johnson Wilkinson, a churchwarden at St John's, Birkby. After him came stockbroker Frederick Bentley and in 1908 the house was modestly extended for Joseph Stork, brother of John Stork at Deveron House and like him a spinner.

Next comes a gap where only the gate piers of a lost house remain. By process of elimination from the Fenton leases and Census information, this was probably built for ironmonger William Ludlam Ramsden and named **Moorcroft**. By the early 1960s it was semi-derelict, reputedly haunted and was soon to be demolished – probably by builder George Haigh to give access to Clayton Fields, which he owned and hoped to develop (see p.83).[184] Between its gate piers one can, for now, still enter the Fields, or indeed exit them having followed the paths down from Bryan Rd (see p.132), though there is no public right of way.

Beyond this point, four of the original Fenton plots were all leased by George Brook junior. On the left are two very large, symmetrical semis (numbered 15 and 16 Queen's Rd), plans for which were submitted by the leading local builders Abraham Graham & Sons; although somewhat stolid, they display attractive decorative motifs in the gables. The first house, once **Laurence Dene(58)**, was home to woollen merchant William Shaw in 1891 and draper Frederick Whitfield in 1911 – presumably the department store owner whose family later moved to Bryan Wood (see p.121). An early occupant of the second house, **Storalee (58)**, was Allen Haigh, woollen merchant and wholesale clothier; he was followed by the accountant W H Armitage, before he built Banney Royd, and by Arthur Crosland, a traveller in wines and spirits, who was there in 1911.

Fig.93
Laurence Dene (left) & Storalee, Queen's Rd.

Across the road is Brook's own home, **Fernbrook (59)**, now 4 Murray Rd, in a free Gothic style with a large pillared porch. The building plans of 1870, somewhat crudely drawn and bearing only Brook's name, suggest that he may have been his own architect, for this and his other houses, in collaboration with builder Abraham Graham. Certainly it was Graham who submitted plans in 1879 for an aquarium and kennel block behind the house, on the bank of Clayton Dike. The site of the outbuildings, with their own entrance, has now been developed as 6 Murray Rd. At the opposite end of the plot, where it meets Blacker Rd, is the smaller **Elm Grove(60)** (now Alexandra House), a more modest house built by Brook as a retirement home for his father, and later occupied by wool merchant Harry Berry. In 1893 the conservatories occupied more space than the house and the pineapple motif above the ground floor window is another indication of Brook senior's horticultural interests.

The Brooks were in fact a most interesting family.[185] The first George Brook (1803–80) was son of James Brook, a local Ramsden estate agent (whose son Joseph and grandson Thomas also held this position).[186] A dyer by training, he worked for the Starkey Brothers at Longroyd Bridge but was dismissed in 1839, with others, on account of his radical socialist views – with Read Holliday, another dyer by trade (see p.47), he was one of the founders of the Owenite Hall of Science in Bath St. As Alan Brooke notes, "this victimisation proved a blessing in disguise since he was forced to establish his own business" at Folly Hall, where other dyeworks operated near to the river. His son George Brook junior (1830–88) received a socialist education at Harmony Hall, Hampshire, one of Owen's experimental co-operative communities, and established his own woollen and worsted business at Larchfield Mills, Firth St, which grew to be a very substantial enterprise with 300 'hands' by 1871 (the buildings are now partly incorporated into the University). He too was associated with the co-operative (and Liberal) cause, and the Co-operative leader George Holyoake is recorded taking supper at Fernbrook in 1877 – "good salmon and good trout"; Brook was a keen angler – after opening the new Co-op at Marsh.[187] George Brook junior's son, also George (1857-93) and often referred to as 'George

Fig.94
Elm Grove, Murray Rd, with pineapple motif.

ter' (or third), was less interested both in industry and politics than his forebears, but became a keen naturalist. Having studied sciences at Owen's College, forerunner of Manchester University (but unconnected with Robert Owen), he was a leading light in the Huddersfield Naturalist Society and the Yorkshire Naturalist Union – hence the purpose-built aquarium at the bottom of the garden. Due perhaps to congenital heart disease, however, all three George Brooks died within 12 years, between 1881 and 1893, and the mill was up for sale in 1901.

Opposite the Brook plot, on the SW side of Murray Rd, are three smaller houses built for leaseholder James Young, a brick manufacturer. Starting from Blacker Rd, **Woodside (61)** was first occupied by woollen salesman Richard Carpenter in the late 1860s and then by his son Edward, an engineer. Next is **Glen Villa (62)**, where engineer William Holmes, founder of W C Holmes, was there in 1881 but Young himself by 1891, with his

Fig.95
Glen Villa, Murray Rd.

family still there in 1911. The last house, unnamed today, was almost certainly **Strathmore** (**63**), probably built in the late 1880s; taken first by George Schofield, 'American merchant', by 1911 it was home to six sisters named Sykes.[188]

Continuing up the hill on the left, and in contrast to these modest villas, much of the land between Murray Rd, Queen's Rd and Blacker Rd was occupied by one very large house and grounds, **Wood Field** (**64**) (listed II), in a stripped-down Tudor style but with attractive details. Emphasising its original scale, today the house is divided into ten flats while the modern housing association development of Woodfield Court provides another 40 or so dwellings in the former grounds. The original Gothic is nicely echoed in a linking block from the house to the modern development.

The original lease, dating from 1869 and perhaps just too early for a building plan to survive, was to landowner Henry Cresswell, and the house, first named Enfield House, was occupied by his younger brother Thomas

Fig.96
Wood Field, Queen's Rd.

Fig.97 (right)
Ellerslie, Queen's Rd.

by 1870. A merchant and Improvement Commissioner, in 1866 he had moved the motion, at a Commissioners' meeting, that initiated the move to incorporate the Borough, achieved in 1868. In the same year, he was also the mover and treasurer of the fund that provided the 'Huddersfield' lifeboat at Happisburgh (Norfolk). But he died in 1872, and by 1877 Wood Field was home to Joseph Armitage Armitage JP. Listed in the 1881 Census as a junior partner in the family woollen business (see p.46), by then J A Armitage was also a property developer who, with surveyor John Henry Hanson (of Holmwood, p.117), went on in the 1880s and 1890s to buy estates at Thornton Lodge, Mold Green and Clough House, Birkby for the development of terraced and back-to-back housing. From 1887 Armitage's own home, in contrast, was The Mansion at Storthes Hall, recently recorded as Huddersfield's most expensive property sale to date.[189] He was followed by George W Tomlinson JP, a Chapel Hill machine maker, better remembered today as secretary of the Yorkshire Archaeological Society, as the first to suggest the Victoria jubilee tower on Castle Hill, and for his extensive notebooks of Huddersfield history, now held by West Yorkshire Archive Service. A later occupier, by 1911, was builder Lewis Radcliffe, of John Radcliffe & Sons.

Across the upper section of Queen's Rd from Wood Field is the equally substantial **Ellerslie (65)** (listed II), which also took up three of the plots originally offered by the Fentons, one now occupied by recent housing. In contrast with its neighbour's pure Tudor, Ellerslie's is an eclectic Gothic design, asymmetric in plan, with elaborate carved decoration and a sharply gabled porch below a three-storey machicholated tower. In this it contrasts with the approved building plan, by Alfred Lofthouse for John Eastwood, which shows a symmetrical double-fronted classical house. Eastwood was indeed the original lessee, in 1873, and a Fenton trustees' minute describes his house as "nearly completed" in 1877.[190] However, it is less clear that he ever occupied it; certainly there is no evidence of occupation in the 1881 Census, by which time Eastwood appears to have been in financial difficulties, and in 1882 the lease was sold to Edwin Learoyd, a printer from Imperial Rd.

Fig.98
Ellerslie, Queen's Rd. The
identity of the carved figures
is unknown.

Learoyd was a son of James Learoyd, Leeds Rd yarn spinner, but married a daughter of Joseph Brook of Glenwood (see p.95) and became a partner in his printing business, which duly became the well-known firm of Brook & Learoyd. He was much involved in the town's sporting life, as a founder of the Cricket & Athletic Club, an early football player at Rifle Fields (which became part of Greenhead Park), and in later life a bowler at Edgerton Park. He died in 1904 but his widow remained until 1913, when the house and grounds were auctioned, together with Learoyd's substantial portfolio of town centre shops and housing. After that the house was occupied by other local businessmen, but from 1950 to 1989 it was in NHS ownership, mostly as a residential training centre for nurses, and is remembered today by many 'Primrose Girls' (cadet nurses) and others who lived there. Today it is in private ownership and provides office accommodation.

In its heyday, Ellerslie was reached via a short drive from Blacker Rd, where the gate piers can still be seen (the present entrance is from Queen's Rd). Between Blacker Rd and the house, this overlooked the Dell, "a superb example of Victorian sunken gardens".[191] Now hopelessly overgrown, these were arranged on several levels, linked by twisting paths and steps, to create picturesque landscape surprises not visible from the house, and the planting is reflected in the floral motifs of the stone carving on the house. Although the result of much landscaping, its origins lay in Blacker Lane Wood, clearly visible on old maps and plans (figs. 3 and 14) with one of Edgerton's north-flowing streams running through it. The Learoyds were evidently keen horticulturalists, also building an orangery and walled garden on extra land added in 1885 and now built on. The deeply incised woodland of the glen gave a magnificent setting to Ellerslie and indeed to Grannum Lodge next door, returning us to the start and providing a fitting – if slightly melancholy – conclusion to the tour.

Notes

1. Derek Linstrum, *West Yorkshire Architects and Architecture* (Lund Humphries, 1978), p.124.

2. Jane Springett, 'Land development and house-building in Huddersfield, 1770–1911', in Martin Doughty (ed), *Building the Industrial City* (Leicester UP, 1986), p.41.

3. George Redmonds, *The Place-Names of Huddersfield* (David Shore, Huddersfield, 2008), p.55.

4. 'A New Look at the Place-name Fartown', *Huddersfield Local History Society [HLHS] Journal*, 2011, pp.26–30. In some early sources Edgerton is rendered as 'Egerton' – we have standardised on Edgerton in this text.

5. The convoluted manorial history of Edgerton has been unpicked, in much greater detail than need concern us, by local historians G W Tomlinson and Philip Ahier. The main sources are Tomlinson Notebooks J and T, respectively KC174/1/8 and KC174/2/3, at West Yorkshire Archive Service – Kirklees (hereafter WYAS-K), and Philip Ahier, 'The story of the manor of Edgerton', *Huddersfield Daily Examiner* (henceforth *HDE*), 22/2/1936. Names associated with the manor from the 13th to 16th centuries are Beaumont, de Edgerton, de Mirfield, Cowper and de Crosland.

6. 'Plan of Huddersfield estate in connexion with book of reference of 1780', WYAS-K, DD/RE.

7. Information in this paragraph is from Gerald Hinchliffe, *A History of King James's Grammar School in Almondbury* (Advertiser Press, Huddersfield, 1963), pp.72–85; Christopher Marsden; George Redmonds; and the deeds referenced in the next note.

8. West Riding Registry of Deeds, CD 574 774 (2–3/11/1778) and CQ 593 855 (17–8/4/1784).

9. Sale notices in *Leeds Intelligencer*, 6/1/1794, 12/10/1801.

10. J C Brook, 'The development of the Edgerton district of Huddersfield during the 19th century' (1979, typescript at Huddersfield Local Studies Library; hereafter JCB); *Leeds Intelligencer*, 22/12/1794; *Leeds Mercury*, 18 & 25/11/1837; recitation of title to Edgerton House, 17/10/1839 (I am grateful to Jeff Lloyd for sight of this).

11. Tomlinson Notebook T, op.cit.

12. This and further details from title deeds to Edgerton Lodge, WYAS-K, C296/240 and Edgerton House (see n.10).

13. JCB; Tomlinson's Notebook Q (WYAS-K, KC174/1/14) and his pedigree of the Hirsts (KC174/2/28).

14. In this they would have been modest examples of the ring of substantial 'villa mansions' circling Huddersfield, built or rebuilt from the 1790s to the 1820s for wealthy landowners and merchants. Nearby examples were Spring Grove and Greenhead Hall, both long demolished, and Rose Hill, Birkby (see p.131), which still stands, much altered. (The 'villa mansion' term is from Linstrum, op.cit. p.81 – intermediate between the country house and the later suburban villa.)

15. Halifax & Huddersfield Turnpike: book of reference to proposed line, 1823 (WYAS – Wakefield, WRT39, Box 1). The distinctions between the three successive road names are thoroughly confused in the 19th century, and part was originally just called 'Edgerton'. For this reason I have quite often referred to today's A629 simply as the 'main road'.

16. Valuation by Abbey, Hanson & Rowe; WYAS-K, KC353/1/3. The plan on p.18 derives from this sale.

17. Alex Brummer & Roger Cowe, *Hanson: A Biography* (Fourth Estate, 1994).

18. *Huddersfield College Magazine*, March 1878.

19. Even then, the survey must have been slightly ahead of the facts on the ground – 'Edgerton Cottage' is apparently the terrace of three small houses linked to Edgerton Hill, not the present house of that name, while 'Edgerton Villa' is apparently today's Cottage, not the Villa further out on the opposite side of the road!

20. E J Law, 'The Bradley family and their Newhouse', *Old West Riding*, 5:2, 1985, pp.22–4.

21. Rate Books at WYAS-K.

22. Letter by 'ER' in the *Huddersfield Chronicle* [hereafter *HC*], 23/1/1858.

23. Tomlinson, 'Pedigree of the Hirsts' (WYAS-K, KC174/2/28). Lockwood himself may have been a son of Joshua Lockwood, the woollen manufacturer with extensive mills in Upperhead Row. This is stated as fact by Tomlinson and in Lockwood's obituary (*Huddersfield Weekly Examiner*, 5/4/1890), but has been questioned by Brian du Feu, who is undertaking current research on the Lockwood family. Certainly Joshua Lockwood came to live at Hazelgrove, which was built on Lockwood land, but there was a Lockwood-to-Lockwood lease, not just a family arrangement (information from William Murgatroyd).

24. Edgerton Cottage and The Mount: original leases inspected, thanks respectively to David Bowen and Robert Sutcliffe. Glenside: sale particulars of 12/7/1881 in Eddisons collection, WYAS-K, B/ETB/sp29.

25. *Huddersfield Weekly Examiner*, 5/4/1890.

26. 'Return of owners of land 1873: Yorkshire West Riding', www.archivecdbooks.org [hereafter '1873 survey'].

27. The account of their history over this and subsequent paragraphs draws on Philip Ahier, 'Story of the Manor of Fixby and its Lords', *HDE*, 16/1/1937 and the Thornhill Estate Acts, 1852–5, available at WYAS-K, C365/45. The Lindley Enclosure Award and map is at WYAS-K, SR2.

28. The date for Fixby Hall, and Carr's involvement, were suggested by the late Alan Petford.

29. While the case ground on, an alternative opportunity presented itself at the end of the 1840s as the town debated the appalling state of the parish church burial ground and the need for a new cemetery. Negotiations between the Thornhill agent J H Ramsbotham and the town's Dissenters identified possible sites on each side of Halifax Rd, either close to Sunny Bank or in today's Kaffir Rd area (Ramsden papers, WYAS-K, DD/RE/C/58–9.) Eventually these schemes were discarded in favour of today's Edgerton Cemetery east of Blacker Rd, which the Improvement Commissioners bought from the Ramsden estate in 1851.

30. Ramsden papers, WYAS-K, DD/RA/C/Box 31.

31. Tolson had inherited this land from his wife's uncle William Armytage, a tanner of Bay Hall (Tomlinson Notebook Q, KC174/4/14). There is no known connection with William Armytage of the original Edgerton settlement (see p.14).

32. Ramsden papers (DD/RA/C/28/5) reveal that the estate, in line with Loch's judgement, thought the land was overpriced and had not authorised Brook's bid. However Brook had apparently colluded with his fellow agent George Crowther, who was acting for both Tolson and Thornhill, to buy on his own account and resell to Thornhill at a profit (perhaps to help Crowther obscure the fact that he was handling both sides of the transaction). Brook was severely reprimanded and narrowly avoided dismissal from the Ramsdens' service. Loch's judgement of Edgerton is cited in Jane Springett, 'Landowners and Housebuilders in the 19th Century', in E A H Haigh (ed), *Huddersfield – A Most Handsome Town* (Kirklees Council, 1992).

33. *HC*, 3, 10 & 24/7/1858. Edgerton Bank, at the apex of the site, is from around 1851 and must have been released earlier, either by the Battye executors, who had retained it in 1839, or by Varley.

34. Fenton Trustee minute books, WYAS-K, C296/82.

35. Fenton papers, WYAS-K, C296/80.

36. Ramsden papers, WYAS-K, DD/RE/C/43.

37. Ramsden papers, WYAS-K, DD/RA/C/9/3, DD/RA/C/37/3.

38. Jane Springett, 'Land development and house-building in Huddersfield, 1770–1911', in Martin Doughty (ed), *Building the industrial city* (Leicester UP, 1986). Springett's work is the most detailed study of 19th century property development in Huddersfield.

39. I am grateful to Roger Lynch for sharing his extensive knowledge of Huddersfield's mining history.

40. These plans, which could be found 20 years ago at the Slaithwaite offices of Carter Jonas, then the agents for Thornhill Yorkshire Estates, have since been lost.

41. A large number of Thornhill estate Edgerton leases are held at WYAS-K, T/L/XII/1–52. There appear to have been two standard versions, in 1855 and 1863.

42. Lease for The Mount, 1850.

43. Lease for Ellerslie, 1883; I am grateful to Anthony Dann for sight of this.

44. Oddly surviving in the Ramsden rather than the Thornhill papers (WYAS-K, DD/RE/86), but the respective estate agents were no doubt keeping close tabs on each other's activities.

45. At Calverley, drives were laid out on a grand scale, again named after the daughters, and four Gothic entrance lodges built, three still standing today, but very few houses followed. Calverley historian Angi Naylor suggests that this was because the estate's location on the South bank of the Aire made it less appealing than the sunnier and more successful Rawdon on the opposite bank. The planned estate can be walked using the published Calverley Loop Bridleway, available at http://west-leeds-country-park-and-green-gateways.webplus.net/calverley_loop_bridleway.html

46. I am grateful to Christopher Marsden for unearthing the Thornhills' service records; Ted Royle for detailing the war; and Edmund Thornhill for confirming the family relationship.

47. *HDE*, 13/1/1882 and information from John Ward.

48. Thornhill papers, WYAS-K, DD/T/R/a/74. This outlay would equate to at least £500,000 in today's prices.

49. *Yorkshire Post*, 15/11/1867; *HC*, 12/2/1870.

50. Thomas Varley's will, WYAS-K, KC642/25. Ramsbotham had recommended Varley as an original trustee of the estate, as the 1852 Act went through Parliament, describing him as "a gentleman who has realised a handsome fortune, is an excellent man of business and is well acquainted with the value of property in this neighbourhood"; but the family preferred to look further afield for their trustees. (Thornhill papers, WYAS-K, DD/T/C/12.)

51. I am grateful to David Verguson for spotting the committee in the 1910 Land Tax returns.

52. Fenton papers, WYAS-K, C296/80.

53. 'Edgerton Conservation Area', Woodhall Planning & Conservation, Leeds, 2007 [hereafter 'ECA review'.]

54. David Wyles, 'Architectural design in C19 Huddersfield', in E A H Haigh (ed) (1992), p.321.

55. Donald Olsen, *The Growth of Victorian London* (Batsford, 1976), p.213. For Edgerton's public transport, see p.61.

56. L Davidoff & C Hall, *Family Fortunes: Men and women of the English middle class, 1780–1850* (Routledge, 1987), p.370.

57. Sale particulars published by Eddisons, estate agents, July 1860. I am grateful to Christine Beacham for sight of these.

58. Thomas Armstrong, *The Crowthers of Bankdam* (Collins, 1940).

59. I was able to attribute Lunnclough Hall to Pritchett in the mid-1990s from the plans submitted to the Thornhill estate, while researching my 'Read Holliday and Lunnclough Hall: a 19th century entrepreneur and his home', in Stephen Wade (ed), *Aspects of Huddersfield 2* (Wharncliffe, 2002), and greatly regret not examining other plans at the time.

60. The Edgerton attributions largely derive from my own research, but for further information about the architects represented, I have relied heavily and gratefully on previous research by Keith Gibson, Edward Law and Christopher Marsden. Confirmed references to tender adverts or building plans appear in the Perambulation section or Table of Houses.

61. Brian Haigh, 'From miserable village to town of great character: from builder to architect', *HLHS Journal* 21, 2009–10

62. It is in answering this question that the earlier research of John Brook comes into its own. His invaluable information on individuals and their lives in Edgerton has been supplemented from a variety of sources, particularly the *Huddersfield Chronicle*, Bachelors Ball minutes (see note 76 below) and the Census. Other specific sources for particular families – often drawn to my attention by Christopher Marsden – are noted separately.

63. The history of the business is set out in Vivien Teasdale, *Huddersfield Mills: A Textile Heritage* (Wharncliffe Books, 2004).

64. Kathleen Brown, 'Edgerton – The elite suburb of Huddersfield and its inhabitants' (1994 typescript lodged at Huddersfield Local Studies Library, BEK900).

65. The genealogy is set out in G M Ward, *A Short History of Milnsbridge House and Surrounding Area* (1982), with further information at http://landedfamilies.blogspot.co.uk/search?q=armitage.

66. Alan Brooke, *The Hall of Science: Co-operation and Socialism in Huddersfield, c.1830–1848* (Workers' History Publications, Honley, 1993), available at https://undergroundhistories.wordpress.com

67. This point is argued at length in David Griffiths, 'Huddersfield in turbulent times, 1815–1850: Who ruled and how?', *Northern History*, LII:1, March 2015.

68. For further information see David Griffiths, *Joseph Brook of Greenhead: 'Father of the Town'* (Huddersfield Local History Society, 2013).

69. Though not to be confused with another leading Commissioner, the wool merchant Joseph Brook of Greenhead, mentioned above; nor with Joseph Brook, Ramsden agent, who was succeeded by his son Thomas, mentioned above.

70. This case has been strongly argued by Tristram Hunt in his *Building Jerusalem: The Rise and Fall of the Victorian City* (Orion, 2004).

71. Brown, op.cit.

72. Judith Flanders, *The Victorian House* (Harper Collins, 2004). The Beeton quotation is cited there, p.79.

73. However George Sheeran suggests that billiard tables may previously have been housed in halls: G Sheeran, *Brass Castles: West Yorkshire New Rich and their Houses, 1800–1914* (Ryburn, 1993), p.63.

74. By John North (*HC*, 28/5/1870) and C H Ronah-Robottom (*HC*, 28/9/1876).

75. *HC*, 6/6/1863, 23/7/1881.

76. For the opportunity to study this, I am most grateful to David Blakeborough.

77. Brown, op.cit.

78. Bretton Hall College, 'Notes on early suburban development in C19 Huddersfield' (1977), available at HLSL. The historian W L Burn, whose study of the years 1852–67 corresponds with Edgerton's development, has suggested that "'Carriage-folk' was a sufficiently exact description of a class in English society." (W L Burn, *The Age of Equipoise*, George Allen & Unwin, 1964, p.17.) When T E Hirst left Willow Bank in 1896, he offered three carriages for sale – a light brougham, a Victoria and a phaeton (*HC*, 4/4/1896).

79. Its minutes are at WYAS-K, KMT18/6/1/1.

80. Ramsden papers, DD/R/dd/VII/109.

81. Its minutes are at WYAS-K, KMT18/9/1/1.

82. This followed the demise of an alternative source of authority – the last recorded meeting of the ratepayers of Marsh hamlet was on 26 March 1866. (Marsh hamlet minute book, WYAS-K, KC788.)

83. Roy Brook, *Huddersfield Corporation Tramways* (1983).

84. *HC*, 22/10/1887, 14/6/1890.

85. *HC*, 18/6/1894.

86. Eddisons collection, WYAS-K, B/ETB/sp/39.

87. WYAS-K, C296/98; *HC*, 3/6/1896.

88. Eddisons collection, WYAS-K, B/ETB/sp/52.

89. A sale plan appears in the deeds of The Mount.

90. The author's annual contribution, for a 1920s semi-detached house, is £7.80.

91. Joseph Sharples, personal communication.

92. The same team was responsible, at the same time, for Station St Buildings in the town centre.

93. *HDE*, 10/9/1959.

94. This was Nikolaus Pevsner's description of Wood in his *Buildings of England: Yorkshire West Riding*, 2nd ed., revised by Enid Ratcliffe (Penguin, 1967, p.275).

95. Here is not the place to analyse Banney Royd in detail. This was splendidly done in *Banney Royd: 'An Agreeable House'*, by the Banney Royd Study Group (Kirklees Council, 1991), still available from Huddersfield Local Studies Library. For Wood's local work generally, see the website of the Edgar Wood Heritage Group (Yorkshire), http://edgarwoodinyorkshire. co.uk/

96. The 'triangle' also included an older house, Inglewood. Right on Long Lane (now Birkby Rd), this is definitely beyond 'Edgerton' but is mentioned for completeness. From at least 1876 until his death in 1902 it was occupied by Frederick Shaw, woollen merchant.

97. Most information in this paragraph comes from the late Edward Law's very useful website, 'Huddersfield & District History', http://homepage.eircom.net/~lawedd/index.htm

98. Thomas Armstrong, *The Crowthers of Bankdam* (Collins, 1940), p.423.

99. For Kaye, http://homepage.eircom.net/~lawedd/ VEHICLEREG.htm. The Liechtenstein owner of Hoyle's Rolls made contact with the Edgar Wood Heritage Group (Yorkshire) in 2014. Joseph Hopkinson at Cleveland House owned a 1905 Daimler when he died in 1907.

100. Tenders, *HC*, 22/8/1868. Crossland's plan for the two houses was the third entry in the new Corporation's building plans register, on 12 January 1869.The circular window (now blind) high above the entrance perhaps owes something to the 'wheel windows' of 17th century Pennine halls, for example Elland New Hall.

101. Edward Law, 'William Henry Crossland, Victorian architect, http://homepage.eircom. net/~lawedd/WHCBLDG1868-71.htm

102. HC , 24/10/1888, 7/11/1888.

103. Gordon & Enid Minter, *Discovering Old Huddersfield*, vol.5 (2002), p.49.

104. *HC*, 3/7/1858, 10/7/1858.

105. Eddisons collection, WYAS-K, B/ETB/sp/39 (10/10/1882).

106. *HC*, 8/2/1862 & 27/12/1862. No inquest was held.

107. *HDE*, 23/3/1968.

108. This has been suggested by Joseph Sharples on the basis of stylistic affinity with Cocking's Market Place bank, now RBS. The odd location of the gate piers, set back from the road line, reflects the pre-turnpike boundary between Fenton and Battye land.

109. I am grateful, here and elsewhere, to Christine Verguson for access to her research on the Sykes family.

110. *HDE*, 9/3/2010.

111. The return of the Armitage name to the C18 Armytage plot is coincidental.

112. Parish Church inscription; Philip Ahier, *The Story of the Three Parish Churches of St Peter the Apostle, Huddersfield* (Advertiser Press, 1948–50), p.278.

113. Building Plan (hereafter BP) H21323 (1933) at WYAS-K

114. It was splendidly restored in 2014 (in time for the Tour de France to pass!) after representations about its declining condition by the Civic Society.

115. There seems to be nothing in the more exotic explanation sometimes advanced, of a connection with Rievaulx Abbey; though the Cistercian abbeys of Byland, Fountains and Rievaulx did all have 'granges' (farms) and mineral interests in the Huddersfield area.

116. This can be seen on the 1888 Ramsden Estate map (WYAS-K, SR2).

117. *HC*, 17/6/1893.

118. *HC*, 22/6/1872.

119. *HC*, 7/2/1857.

120. He should not be confused with his namesake the wool merchant Joseph Brook (p.48), whom he replaced on the HIC in 1855.

121. *HDE*, 4/2/1915.

122. 'Art & Art-Cultivation in England', Pt X, *HC*, 5/12/1857. This 17-part series of anonymous articles, perhaps by the local artist G D Tomlinson, includes extensive observations on the town's buildings, but comes a little too early to have a great deal to say about Edgerton – though there are positive judgements of Willow Bank and Hazelgrove.

123. Eddisons collection, WYAS-K, B/ETB/sp29, 12/7/1881.

124. Thornhill papers, DD/T/C/274, DD/T/L/XII/33.

125. A B Brown, 'Site at rear of 4A Cleveland Rd, Edgerton', Woodhall Planning & Construction, 2007.

126. *HC*, 16/4/1864. However sale particulars of 1876 reveal Sunny Bank, presumably on a reduced plot, to be a well-appointed five-bedroom house (*HC*, 24/6/1876).

127. *HC*, 9/5/1885.

128. Sale particulars, HLHS, BEK728.3.

129. G Sheeran, *Brass Castles: West Yorkshire New Rich and their Houses, 1800–1914* (Ryburn, 1993).

130. *HDE*, 19/8/2015.

131. This is speculation, but we know that in the 1890s Briarcourt in Occupation Rd, Lindley was commissioned from Edgar Wood, himself a member of the Sykes family, as a wedding present for Herbert Higginson Sykes and his wife.

132. *HC*, 14 & 21/10/1886.

133. *HC*, 24/8/1895.

134. Though apparently not the same man, confusingly, as the wool merchant Joseph Turner who leased and sub-let all three plots. Living in New North Rd, the latter was a leading light in the Improvement Commissioners, Waterworks Commissioners and Infirmary.

135. A "newly erected mansion opposite Oakwood" was advertised for auction by "John Eastwood, architect" in the *HC*, 1/10/1864; though he was primarily a builder.

136. Although Granville is at the bottom of my garden, I am grateful to Christopher Marsden for discovering its architectural history.

137. Philip Ahier, *St Peter's*, p.262

138. WYAS-K, SR2.

139. This information is largely from Hugh Wright Mellor, 'Wright Mellor of Huddersfield', *HLHS Newsletter*, 10:1990.

140. *HC*, 22/3/1862, 26/7/1862, 3/1/1863.

141. Pamela Cooksey, *Public Lives: The Family of Joseph Woodhead* (HLHS, 1999).

142. *HDE*, cited in Clyde Binfield, *So Down to Prayers: Studies in English Nonconformity, 1780–1920* (Dent, 1977), p.158.

143. They invited tenders on 31/3/1866 for an unnamed house at Edgerton, and on 25/5/1867 for an enlargement and lodge for J H Taylor, the owner of Ravensdeane (both references from *HC*).

144. *Yorkshire Evening Post*, 10/6/1913.

145. Salomons & Steinthal to Richard Dugdale, Borough Surveyor, 3/12/1888, filed with BP L746 (1889).

146. Obituary, *HDE*, 6/6/1931.

147. The dating is clear from the Thornhill estate lease, T/L/XII/43, but I have not been able to find a building plan and hence an architect.

148. The cottage behind is by Dawson & Jones, builders and joiners, of Mold Green – better known for putting up circus stages!

149. Hughes also designed the stables, coach house and cottage, added in 1881

150. Brown, 1994.

151. Vivien Hirst, *Family of Four: A Remembrance of Childhood* (Raymond Prior, 1993).

152. *HDE*, 8/7/1957.

153. Cooper also added a new stables and coach house in 1895.

154. According to memorials of the original deeds at WY Deeds Registry, inspected by John Brook, Holliday originally named Woodlands Queen's Villa, while Hollinhurst was Park Villa and Holmwood was Otley House. However there is no evidence that these names were adopted by the leaseholders.

155. Jill Liddington, *Rebel Girls: Their fight for the vote* (Virago, 2006).

156. These can be found on the BBC website at http://www.bbc.co.uk/arts/yourpaintings/artists/samuel-howell.

157. Anne C Brook, 'Looking to the Future: Huddersfield Chamber of Commerce Year Book 1918', *HLHS Journal* 27, 2016/17.

158. *HDE*, 4/5/1946.

159. *Yorkshire Post* 2/11/1951.

160. HC, 23/5/1885; Eddisons collection, WYAS-K, B/ETB/sp52 – sale of freehold ground rents, 12/3/1889. Fisher is not to be confused with Henry Fischer of The Knowle, partner of Edward Huth next door at Oakfield.

161. Vivien Teasdale, *Huddersfield Mills: A Textile Heritage* (2004), p.41.
162. Black dyeing was difficult, tending to produce greys, so the 'black dyer' was a respected specialist trade.
163. Obituary, *HC*, 4/1/1892.
164. B Moriarty, 'Politics and Education in Huddersfield in the Late 19th Century', in Haigh (1992), pp.527–60.
165. *HC*, 10/3/1890.
166. *Yorkshire Post*, 12/8/1927, 2/1/1929.
167. *HC*, 6/7/1899.
168. The Beaumont story is detailed in David Griffiths, *Huddersfield's Best Address: Four Centuries of Life at Greenhead Hall* (Friends of Greenhead Park, 2015).
169. Sheeran, *Brass Castles*, p.114.
170. Christopher Marsden has identified that the records of Stocks, Sykes & Hickson contained several documents, now destroyed, re Stoneleigh.
171. Thornhill papers, T/DD/XII/6; BP M806.
172. Clyde Binfield, op.cit., p.176.
173. *British Architect*, 20/2/1891.
174. This can be viewed on the Historic England website, at http://archive.historicengland.org.uk (search on Stoneleigh Huddersfield).
175. Information from Stan Driver: the conversion of coach houses to 'motor houses' was a feature of the early C20.
176. Borough Architect's plans, WYAS-K, CBH/A/670, 1949. The figure of 23 residents (all female) is from the 1953 electoral register.
177. Peter Cardno, *Past Artists of Huddersfield* (1923).
178. I am grateful to Norma Hardy for this information.
179. Although no plan has been found, it seems the best candidate for Kirk's tender in the *HC*, 17/6/1871.
180. *HC*, 20/3/1895.
181. Gordon & Enid Minter, *Discovering Old Huddersfield*, vol.1 (1993), p.13.
182. Fenton papers, WYAS-K, C296/80.
183. These houses are likely to match Abbey's tenders for "two semi-detached villas in Murray Road on Fenton's Estate, near Edgerton", *HC*, 28/8/1869. The identification of houses in this area is complicated by the redesignation of some from Murray Rd to Queen's Rd.
184. I am grateful to Simon Goodyear and William Murgatroyd for these recollections.
185. For most of the following information I am indebted to Alan Brooke, 'The Brooks of Larchfield Mill', available at https://undergroundhistories.wordpress.com/
186. Thomas is not to be confused with his namesake the solicitor at Bryan Rd, but did live nearby at Mayfield (p.78).
187. *HC*, 1/6/1877.
188. Young submitted plans for 4 houses all told – BPs M64 (1870) and M84 (1871) by John Eastwood, for one and two villas respectively, and BP M676 (1887) for a further villa, by Joseph Berry.
189. Details of Armitage's career from Jane Springett, 'Landowners and Housebuilders in the 19th Century', in E A H Haigh (ed)(1992); *HDE*, 4/2/2016 for the record 2015 property sale.
190. Fenton papers, WYAS-K, C296/80,82.
191. Jim MacDonald, Kirklees Council trees officer, quoted in *HDE*, 29/11/1990.

Table of Houses

NAME	MAP NO. (a)	MODERN ADDRESS	DATE (b)	BUILDING PLANS (c) *LISTING NOS (d)*	SEE PAGES (e)
Ashfield House – see Roseneath					
Ashleigh	30	9 Halifax Rd	1863	L2011 (1901), L2728 (1905) *1134177* *1212945* *1313881*	**107–8**
Bankfield	4	12 Edgerton Rd	1863	*1134247*	29, 69, **79–80**
Bankfield	52	4 Queen's Rd	1870	**M23(1869)**	**132–3**
Banney Royd	–	Banney Royd Hall, HD3 3BJ	1902	**L819 (1900)** *1134184*	**66–7**, 69, 71, 147
Beechwood	49	8–9 Bryan Rd	1860	M673 (1887) *1134334–6*	46, 54, **125–6**
Binham Lodge – see Thornleigh	46				
Brantwood (originally Woodbine)	40	24 Kaffir Rd	1866	*1134173* *1288944*	34, 53, **118**
Bremen House (once West Lodge)	6	16 Edgerton Rd	1868	M13 (1869) *1134248–9*	62, **81–2**
Bryan Croft	41	26 Kaffir Rd	1925	H14301 (1924)	**118–9**
Bryan Lodge – see Woodleigh	47				
Bryan Wood (originally Brooklyn)	44	1 Bryan Rd	1863		50, **120–1**, 131, 135

NAME	MAP NO. (a)	MODERN ADDRESS	DATE (b)	BUILDING PLANS (c) *LISTING NOS (d)*	SEE PAGES (e)
Buckden Mount	34	8 Thornhill Rd	1873	**L45 (1872 – missing),** L137 (1876), L319 (1880) *1239741* *1273673*	69, **112–3**
Burbank	33	12 Thornhill Rd	1875	*1239750* *1273674*	82, **111–2**
Burleigh House	7	1 Queen's Rd	1865	*1278106*	**82**
Burnieside	54	8 Queen's Rd	1885		**133**
Cedar Grove	45	3 Binham Rd	1870	**M9 (1869),** L201 (1876)	71, **121–2**
Cleveland House	21	2 Cleveland Rd	1863	*1134330* *1313834*	37, 56–7, **96–7**
Clyde House	4	10 Edgerton Rd	1863	*1134246/7*	29, **79–80**
Cote Royd	29	7 Halifax Rd	1862	L27 (1870), L87 (1874) *1134220–1* *1212916*	**106–7**
Deveron House	53	7 Queen's Rd	1906	**H2746 (1905)**	68, **133**
Edgerton Bank	5	14 Edgerton Rd	1851	M821 (1889)	49, **80–1,** 145
Edgerton Cottage	10	15 Edgerton Rd	1849	*1134947*	23, 26, 49, **86,** 144
Edgerton Grove	–	Demolished	c1820		17, 18, **19–20,** 68
Edgerton Hill	8	7 Edgerton Rd	c1820	L309 (1880), M473 (1883) *1134254*	**18–21,** 46, 69, **82–3,** 86
Edgerton House	–	Demolished	c1820		**19–20,** 28, 79–80, 86
Edgerton Lodge	–	Demolished	c1820		**19**
Edgerton Villa	16	24 Edgerton Rd	1850	*1134253* *1211965*	23, **93,** 99, 144

NAME	MAP NO. (a)	MODERN ADDRESS	DATE (b)	BUILDING PLANS (c) *LISTING NOS (d)*	SEE PAGES (e)
Ellerslie	65	Queen's Rd	1878	**M218 (1877)** *1220505* *1313784*	**139–42**
Elm Crest (originally Elm Lea)	7	2 Queen's Rd	1865	*1278106*	**82**
Elmford	57	12 Queen's Rd	1876		**135**
Elm Grove	60	2 Murray Rd	1871		**136**
Fernbrook	59	4 Murray Rd	1871	**M52 (1870), M303 (1879)** *1228184–5*	**136**
Fernleigh (now Thornleigh)	33	10 Thornhill Rd	1875	*1239750*	**111–2**
Gables, The	32	3 Thornhill Rd	1890	**L746 (1889)**	**109–10**
Glenside	18	Demolished	1856		26, 40, 62, **95–6**
Glen View	19	5/7 Cleveland Rd	1864		40, **96**
Glen Villa	62	3 Murray Rd	1870		**137–8**
Glenwood	17	2/2A Halifax Rd	1856	L357 (1880), L392 (1881), L468 (1883), H10479 (1912) *1134179*	40, **94–5**
Grange, The	43	4 Halifax Rd	1861	*1134180–3*	48, 71, **119–20**
Grannum Lodge & House	3	6/6A Edgerton Rd	1864	*1134244* *1313873*	29, 30, 74–5, 78–9
Granville	26	5 Hungerford Rd	1875	M147 (1874)	**104–5**
Hazeldene/Hazelgrove – see Waverley	15				
Hollinhurst	38	12 Kaffir Rd	1868	*1134170* *1213697*	**117, 149**
Holly Bank	56	10 Queen's Rd	1865–70		**134**
Holmwood (once Bythewood Hollow)	38	14 Kaffir Rd	1868	*1134171* *1313877*	**117, 140, 149**

NAME	MAP NO. (a)	MODERN ADDRESS	DATE (b)	BUILDING PLANS (c) / *LISTING NOS (d)*	SEE PAGES (e)
Hungerford House	23	5 Halifax Rd	1855	L712 (1888) *1212897* *1313861*	102–3
Knowle, The (once Holly Mount)	14	21 Edgerton Rd	1852	*1313836*	40, 50, 88–9
Laurel Bank (once Bryancliffe)	25	3 Hungerford Rd	1864	*1134158–9* *1313913*	102–3
Laurence Dene	58	15 Queen's Rd	1881	M344/54 (1880)	135
Low Wood (formerly Coverdale)	42	28 Kaffir Rd	1925	H14651 (1924)	118–9
Lunnclough Hall	37	6/8 Kaffir Rd	1856	L798 (1889) *1134169* *1134172* *1313876*	41, 93, 94, 115–7, 146
Marsh Field	2	5 Edgerton Rd	1869		76–7
Mayfield	3	8 Edgerton Rd	1864	*1134245* *1313874*	29, 30, 74–5, 78–9
Moorcroft	–	Demolished	1870		135
Mount, The	13	1 & 2 The Mount, Edgerton Rd	1850	*1134255*	26, 88–9
Norwood	–	Demolished	1892	L905 (1891), L654 (1899), L717 & 717a (1899), 829 (1900), 891 (1900).	62, 63–6
Oak Hill	1	1 Edgerton Grove Rd	1869		71, 76–7
Oak Lea	11	9 Regent Rd	1870	M30 (1869) *1277382* *1231776*	87
Oakfield Lodge	48	6 Bryan Rd	By 1860		125
Oakleigh	40	20/22 Kaffir Rd	1866	*1288944* *1313878*	117–8
Oakley House	24	1 Hungerford Rd	1860	L412 (1882) *1134157* *1313912*	102–3

NAME	MAP NO. (a)	MODERN ADDRESS	DATE (b)	BUILDING PLANS (c) *LISTING NOS (d)*	SEE PAGES (e)
Oakwood	28	2 Hungerford Rd	1863	*1134154–5*	**38–9,** 68–9, **105**
Ravensdeane	31	1 Thornhill Rd	1867	L63 & 69 (1873), L634 (1877) *1239524* *1239760–1*	51, 69, **109**
Rose Bank	12	17 Edgerton Rd	1851	*1211985*	87
Roseneath	12	1 Luther Place	1851	*1215703*	45, 87
Rose Hill	51	161 Birkby Rd	c.1800?	*1134389* *1220401*	**131–2**
Sedgefield	55	9 Queen's Rd	1873	*1231463* *1278109*	42, **133–4**
Somerville	27	4 Hungerford Rd	1863	*1134156* *1313911*	70, **104–5**
Springfield	52	3 Queen's Rd	1870	M23 (1869)	**132–3**
Springfield	36	2 Thornhill Rd	1863	*1239520* *1273672*	**113–4**
Stoneleigh	50	10 Bryan Rd	1860	M520 (1884), M658 (1886), H9425 (1910), H9749 (1911) *1134337*	51–2, 54–5, 67, 71, **126–31**
Storalee	58	16 Queen's Rd	1881	**M344/54 (1880)**	135
Strathmore	63	5 Murray Rd	1888	**M676 (1887)**	138
Sunny Bank	20	4 Cleveland Rd	c.1800?	*1210531*	97
Thorn Hill	35	6 Thornhill Rd	1876	**L108 (1875),** L367 (1881) *1239521* *1239732*	113
Thornleigh	46	7/9 Bryan Rd	1870		62, 112, **122**
Trafford House	30	11 Halifax Rd	1863	*1134178*	**107–8**

NAME	MAP NO. (a)	MODERN ADDRESS	DATE (b)	BUILDING PLANS (c) *LISTING NOS (d)*	SEE PAGES (e)
Waverley (originally Hazeldene/Hazelgrove)	15	18/20 Edgerton Rd	1852	M210 & M230 (1877), M961 (1893), H10477 (1912) *1134251–2*	69, **90–3**
West Mount	2	3 Edgerton Grove Rd	1869		**76–7**
Westoe	56	11 Queen's Rd	1865–70		**134–5**
Willow Bank	22	1 Halifax Rd	1855	L1073 (1896) *1134218–9* *1212865* *1289328* *1313860*	34, 95, 96, **98–101**, 147
Wood Field	64	Queen's Rd	1869	*1231466–7*	138/40
Woodbine – see Brantwood	40				
Woodlands	39	16 Kaffir Rd	1868	*1213705*	**117–8**, 149
Woodleigh	47	Alwoodleigh, 2/4 Bryan Rd	1862		118, **123–4**
Woodside	61	1 Murray Rd	1867		**137–8**
Woodville	14	19 Edgerton Rd	1852	*1313836*	**88–9**

(a)   'Map number' refers to the map on pp.84–85.

(b)   Different dates are available for different properties – for the original lease, approved Building Plan, press report, etc. Those shown here are a 'best guess' at the date of completion and first occupation.

(c)   Dates refer to approval dates rather than completions. The building plans shown in **bold** are for the house itself, down to 1914; the remainder are for alterations, additions, out-buildings etc. They are prefixed L for Lindley, M for Marsh, H for Huddersfield as a finding aid. The plans are held at West Yorkshire Archive Service, Kirklees.

(d)   National Heritage List 7-digit entry numbers (in *italic*), including associated listed lodges, stables, gate piers etc. Where items are grouped together in the table, this need not imply they are in combined ownership today. The National Heritage List, giving a description of the property ('the listing'), is at https://historicengland.org.uk/listing/the-list/

(e)   The principal reference is in **bold**.

Index

For HOUSES see preceding table. Below are NAMES (other than architects), ARCHITECTS and SUBJECTS.

Names (excluding architects)

Abbey, Sidney 81
Anders, Henry 88, 122
Aked, Thomas 79
Armitage
    Alfred 83
    Charles Ingram 46, 123
    George 46, 57
    Joseph 46, 50
    Joseph Armitage 46, 140
    Joseph Taylor 46
    William Henry 66, 67, 135
Armytage, William 14, 145

Barker
    George 107
    Henry 76
Barnicot
    John 97
    Richard 133
Batley
    George Lewis 82
    Joseph 49

Battye, John 17–9
Beaumont
    Edward 126
    John 134
Bentley, Frederick 135
Berry
    Harry 136
    Misses 87
Blackburn, Alfred 88
Brierley, Sydney 93, 107
Broadbent, Horace 20, 68
Brook
    Ada 88
    Arthur 93
    George, snr, jnr & ter 135–7
    George Henry 19, 49, 86, 117
    George Smith 86
    Herbert Smith 55, 87–8
    Joseph (bookseller) 50, 95, 141
    Joseph (wool merchant) 48, 131
    Revd Samuel 12–15
    Thomas (agent) 28, 49, 79, 145
    Thomas (solicitor) 49, 123

Brooke, Edward 102, 103
Bruce, Edward 111
Bull, Henry 88
Burman, James 34, 118

Cameron, Robert 93, 131
Carpenter, Richard 137
Casson, Benjamin 80
Clarke, Dr William 79
Clough, Thomas 20
Cresswell
    Henry 138
    Thomas 138–40
Crosland
    Arthur 135
    James 92
    Joseph, Sir 80
Crowther
    Alfred 92
    George 29, 33, 49, 113, 145
    Godfrey 92, 131
    John Edward 99
    Joseph Hilton 108
    William Alfred 83, 88

Cumming Bell
    Anne 122
    Major 122

Dawson, Mary 87
Dyson
    Hyram 92
    Richard 77

Eastwood
    Frederick 113
    James 82
    John 140
Ellis, Frederick 82
Exley, John 117

Fell, Robert 70, 105
Firth
    Elizabeth 14
    William 107
Fischer, Henry 89
Fisher
    Edward 123
    Edward William 125
Fletcher, Archibald 92
Fox, Joseph 62–3, 66
Freeman
    Charles 68, 105
    John 80, 105

Gilderdale, Revd John 19
Greenwood
    Albert 93
    Frank 93
    Col Frederick 19
    John Brooke 89
Grist, John 118

Haigh
    Allen 135
    Ben 118
    George 83, 135
    Henry 87

    John 83
    Revd John 89
Hall, Anne 71
Hanson
    James, Lord 20, 66
    James (schoolmaster) 93
    John 117
Heywood, William 89
Hinchliffe, James 96
Hirst
    George Crowther 133
    James 80
    John 82
    John, Joseph & Thomas 13, 14,
    17, 25
    Rachel 117
    Thomas (wool merchant) 34,
    93, 96, 99
    Thomas Edward 99, 127, 147
Hoerle, George 118

Holliday
    Read 47, 94, 115–7, 136
    Robert 20
    Thomas 115, 117
Holroyd, Frederick 89
Holmes
    Percy 112, 119
    William 137
Hopkinson
    Abraham 80
    Edith 56–7
    Frank Addy 68, 99
    Joseph 96–7, 148
Hordern, Isaac 20
Howell, Samuel 50, 121, 131
Hoyle, Sir Emmanuel 67
Hudson
    Frederick 17–19, 83
    Thomas 102
Huth
    Edward 125
    Marion 125

Ibbotson, Derek 119

Johnson, Charles 93

Kaye
    Alfred 81
    Joseph Henry, Sir 65–6, 67, 71,
    93, 127
    Lady 63
    Thomas 133
    Tom Herbert 83, 96
    William Johnson 117
Keighley, Charles 92
Knight
    Camille Bernard 110
    George 123

Lancaster, Martha 134
Langton, Frederick 117
Last, Edwin 88
Learoyd
    Edwin 140–2
    Frank 99
    Frederick 118
    Robert 81
    Samuel Turner 126
    Thomas 79
Liddell
    Henry & John (shoemakers) 88
    John (manufacturer) 112
Liebmann, Maximilian 97
Liebreich
    James 19, 80
    Joseph 80
Lockwood
    George 25–6, 32–3, 63, 144
    Joshua 92, 144
Lodge, Joah 79
Lowenthal
    Bertha 71, 120
    Charles 120
    Joseph 48, 120
Lumb, Joe 131–2

Maddock, Revd Henry 19
Mallinson
    Edward 82
    Revd Joel 96
Marsden, John 125
Martin
    Ernest 67
    Henry 46, 125, 127–30
    Horace 46, 125, 127
    Janet 88
    John 131
    John William 97
    Patrick 45, 87, 112
Mellor
    Thomas 118
    Wright 106–7
Middlemost
    Henry 80
    Livingstone 133–4
Midgley, David 113–4
Mills
    Charles 62, 122
    Joseph 93
Moore, William 117–8
Moorhouse, Ambrose 133

Naylor, Thompson 109
Newhouse, Richard 19
Nield, William 132
Norris, Sidney 20
Norton, George Pepler 134–5

Owen, Robert 93

Parratt, Henry 76–7
Pesel, George 122
Pitt, George 102

Radcliffe
    Joseph & William 134
    Lewis 140
Ramsden
    Ludlam 123
    William Ludlam 135

Rhodes, Richard 81
Riley, Jeremiah 131
Rippon, William 121
Roberts, Alfred 102
Robinson
    Frederick 123, 126
    Thomas 83

Schofield
    George 138
    Joshua 131
Shaw
    Foster 89, 102
    G W 82
    Joseph 95
    William 62, 135
Skilbeck, Robert 79
Spivey, Robert 86
Stewart, John 122
Stork
    John 133
    Joseph 135
Susmann, Jacob 20
Sykes
    Alfred 77
    Charles Frederick 95
    Edward Grocock 82
    Ellen 82
    Frederick 117
    James Nield 60, 99
    Jane 99
    John H 103
    Joseph 99
    Misses 138
    William 82, 95

Taylor
    Ephraim Beaumont 92, 121
    Henry 89
    Henry Beaumont 109
    John 109
Tolson, Joshua 28, 33
Tomlinson, George 140

Turner
    Joseph 149
    Joseph Brooke 103

Varley, Thomas 19, 28–30, 34, 146

Waddington, James 89
Walker
    Arthur 65
    Frank 80
    Frederick 82
    John William 82
Wallace, James 77
Watkinson
    James 125
    Thomas 125
Wheatley
    Charles 133
    Joseph 133
    William 133
Whitaker, James 96
Whiteley, William 89, 112
Whitfield, Frederick 135
Whitworth, Joshua 89
Wilkinson, Johnson 135
Willans, James 82, 107–8, 127, 131
Wilson, Thomas 83
Wimpenny, William 107, 122
Woodhead
    Arthur Longden 133
    Edward Booth 53, 107–8
Wrigley, Joseph 79

Young, James 137

Zossenheim
    Julius 81
    Maximilian 80

Architects & Designers

Abbey, Frank 95
Abbey, John Henry 63,
    134
Abbey & Hanson 66, 129
Armitage, George
    Faulkner 44, 99, 101,
    127–30, 131

Bamford, Denis 127, 129
Bamford, Edmund 127
Berry, Joseph 119, 150

Calvert & Jessop 118–9
Cocking
    John William 95
    William 43, 81
Cooper, Willie 44, 92,
    115, 133
Crossland, W H 43, 76–7

Dawson & Jones 149

Eastwood, John 43, 103,
    107, 150

Fowler, Charles 104

Harbron, G Dudley 107
Hatchard Smith, John 66
Healey, Thomas &
    Francis 113
Hughes, Edward 44, 83,
    94, 113

Kirk, John & Sons 42–3,
    65, 76, 78, 82, 87,
    91, 103, 106, 109,
    121–2, 132, 133

Lockwood & Mawson
    109
Lofthouse, Alfred 140
Lunn, John 99

Marsh, Jones & Cribb
    128–9

Nicholson, Ralph 107

W Pontey & Son 33
Portable Building Co 107
Pritchett, J P & Sons
    28, 42, 78, 115–6

Radcliffe, James 50, 89
Robinson, Paul 106

Salomons & Steinthal 110
Stocks, Ben 43, 95, 107,
    109, 125, 127

Tarn, Edward Wyndham
    43, 80

White, Oswald 118
Wood, Edgar & Sellers,
    J H 66, 127, 131, 135

Subjects

Architects 42–4 (see opposite for individuals)

Bachelors' Balls 54–5

Calverley 33, 131, 145
Cars 71, 121, 125, 129
Cemetery 57, 144
Clayton Fields 24, 83, 96, 135
Clubs and societies 54
Coal mining 32

Demolitions 19, 26, 66, 96, 97, 130, 135

Edgerton
    Conservation Area 6–7, 37
    Early settlement 11
    Landscape 14–15, 40
    Manor 11
    Placename 11
    Park 34, 36, 114
Electricity 62

Fenton estate & family 10, 12–3, 29, 32, 33, 34, 63
Funerals 57

Gardens 40–1, 53–4
Gas 60, 61, 62
German merchants 48
Glebe land 86

Highfields 23–4
Huddersfield
    Chamber of Commerce 9
    College 93, 108, 115
    Corporation 51, 59, 61, 62
    Improvement Commissioners 9, 50, 59–60, 86
    School Board 51
    Town FC 108

Land ownership 24–31
Leasehold tenure 31–6
Lindley Enclosure Award 14, 76
Lindley Local Board 60

Manufacturers 45–8
Marriages 56–7
Marsh Local Board 60–1
Merchants 48–9
'Moorheaton' 41
Music 54

New North Road 24, 28, 60
Norwood estate 62–6

Occupations 45–50, 68

Postal service 61–2

Ramsden estate 11–13, 20, 28, 31–2, 46, 60, 75, 145
Recreation 53–4
Religion 51

Schools 19, 51, 77, 88, 90, 93, 118, 121
Servants 51–2, 68–9
Sunny Bank Beck & Glen 14, 40

Telephone service 62
Thornhill estate & family 11, 14, 24, 26–8, 32, 33–6, 63, 105, 121, 131
Trams 61
Turnpike road 20, 60, 93

Water 60
Waverley School 86, 90, 93
Women 51, 125

Huddersfield Civic Society

HUDDERSFIELD CIVIC SOCIETY encourages high standards of architecture and town planning in Huiddersfield. We strive to stimulate public interest and pride in caring for the town and its existing buildings, encourage improvements in its environment and amenities and promote the town as a vibrant and attractive place to live and work.

The Society is dedicated both to preserving and celebrating our built heritage. We are consulted by Kirklees Council, on matters such as proposed alterations to, or demolition of buildings which are "listed" or are in Conservation Areas.

We are not simply a preservation body and spend as much time looking forward as looking back, demonstrated by our annual Design Awards for the town's best new developments. We welcome new buildings of quality which are in sympathy with their surroundings.

We organise, lectures, debates, walks, tours. We support Heritage Open Days and we judge and give the annual Peter Stead Award for sustainable architecture for University of Huddersfield students.

Publications include *The Buildings of Huddersfield: Five Architectural Walks*, *The Old Yards of Huddersfield* and a range of leaflets.

We welcome new members, both as individuals and corporate bodies.

www.huddersfieldcivicsociety.org.uk
info@huddersfieldcivicsociety.org.uk
🐦 @CivicSocietyHD
f @HuddersfieldCivicSociety
Registered Charity Number: 242397

Picture Credits

DAVID GRIFFITHS IS a local historian specialising in 19th century Huddersfield, especially its ruling elites and the development of the public realm. Active in Huddersfield Local History Society, Discover Huddersfield and the Edgar Wood Heritage Group, he has four previous local titles to his name, including a history of Greenhead Park. He is a retired local government officer and has lived in Edgerton since 1989.

ANDREW CAVENEY IS a professional photographer, www.creativedigitalphotography.co.uk. Having graduated with a BA (Hons) in Photography in 1988, he specialises in commercial and architectural photography. His work can be seen in many publications including *Pevsner Architectural Guide; Yorkshire West Riding: Sheffield and the South 2017*. He lives in Birkby, Huddersfield. Away from photography he is the Secretary of the Huddersfield & District Beekeeping Association.

Cover photos:
front, Bremen House, Edgerton Rd.
back, glass of the stairwell bay window, Laurel Bank, Hungerford Rd.